PREVENTION IN PSYCHOLOGY

Other Books in the Prevention Practice Kit

Program Development and Evaluation in Prevention (9781452258010)

Prevention and Consultation (9781452257990)

Best Practices in Prevention (9781452257976)

Prevention Groups (9781452257983)

Public Policy and Mental Health (9781452258027)

Evidence-Based Prevention (9781452258003)

Social Justice and Culturally Relevant Prevention (9781452257969)

Robert Conyne: *To my family: Lynn, Suzanne and Pete, Zack, and our dog Lucy.*
Arthur Horne: *To Gayle*
Katherine Raczynski: *To Kevin*

PREVENTION IN PSYCHOLOGY

An Introduction to the Prevention Practice Kit

ROBERT K. CONYNE
University of Cincinnati

ARTHUR M. HORNE
University of Georgia

KATHERINE RACZYNSKI
University of Georgia

Los Angeles | London | New Delhi
Singapore | Washington DC

Los Angeles | London | New Delhi
Singapore | Washington DC

FOR INFORMATION:

SAGE Publications, Inc.
2455 Teller Road
Thousand Oaks, California 91320
E-mail: order@sagepub.com

SAGE Publications Ltd.
1 Oliver's Yard
55 City Road
London EC1Y 1SP
United Kingdom

SAGE Publications India Pvt. Ltd.
B 1/I 1 Mohan Cooperative Industrial Area
Mathura Road, New Delhi 110 044
India

SAGE Publications Asia-Pacific Pte. Ltd.
3 Church Street
#10-04 Samsung Hub
Singapore 049483

Acquisitions Editor: Kassie Graves
Editorial Assistant: Elizabeth Luizzi
Production Editor: Brittany Bauhaus
Copy Editor: QuADS Prepress (P) Ltd.
Typesetter: C&M Digitals (P) Ltd.
Proofreader: Jeff Bryant
Indexer: Diggs Publication Services, Inc.
Cover Designer: Glenn Vogel
Marketing Manager: Lisa Sheldon Brown
Permissions Editor: Adele Hutchinson

Copyright © 2013 by SAGE Publications, Inc.

Printed in the United States of America

Library of Congress Cataloging-in-Publication Data

Prevention in psychology : an introduction to the prevention practice kit / editors, Robert K. Conyne, Arthur M. Horne, Katherine A. Raczynski.

p. cm. — (Prevention practice kit)
Includes bibliographical references and index.

ISBN 978-1-4522-5795-2 (pbk.)

1. Medicine, Preventive—Psychological aspects.
2. Health promotion—Psychological aspects.
I. Conyne, Robert K. II. Horne, Arthur M., 1942-
III. Raczynski, Katherine A.

RA427.8.P745 2013
616.89—dc23   2012040369

This book is printed on acid-free paper.

12 13 14 15 16 10 9 8 7 6 5 4 3 2 1

Brief Contents _____

Detailed Contents _____

Acknowledgments_____

We thank Kim Bolen for her organizational and editorial work on the project and all the students at our two universities who have contributed over the decades to understanding and applying prevention, and Kassie Graves, our editor at SAGE, for her constant support and helpful guidance. Also, Andy and Kat give special thanks to Pamela Orpinas for her collegial contributions to our prevention efforts over the years. We all thank the Prevention Section members of the Society of Counseling Psychology in the American Psychological Association for their support and innovations. Most of all, our appreciation goes to the teachers, the administrators, the students, and the families, who have contributed so much to our understanding of the value and purpose of early prevention work.

1

The Importance of Prevention

All things considered, it is more desirable to prevent a bad occurrence rather than to treat it after the fact. The maxim, "an ounce of prevention is worth a pound of cure," captures this proactive way of thinking.

Indeed, a growing body of literature is amassing to support a prevention mind-set in psychology and in the broader area of mental health, and many of those sources will be cited in the pages to follow. Yet there remains a need for the development of resources that take direct aim at how to practically apply prevention research and theory to create effective programs that can delay, stop, or reduce conditions leading to mental health disorders.

This first book in the *Prevention Practice Kit* will provide an overview of the prevention field, of the *Kit* contents, and it will highlight key points emerging through the historical evolution of prevention. (*Note:* At the end of this book, we highlight each of the other seven books in the *Kit*.) It will give special attention to elements that will be infused throughout all chapters: a systemic, ecological approach and community and multidisciplinary collaboration. Essential competencies needed for delivering prevention programs will be identified, such as the collaborative attitude and skills necessary to cross boundaries between health and mental health professionals and between scientific and community experts. All this attention to prevention concepts and skills will culminate in an extensive application of prevention focused on bullying, so that you can see an illustration of how prevention practice can occur. Finally, to further boost applied practice, examples are sprinkled throughout the book accompanied by a set of learning exercises. An extensive set of references concludes the book.

So let's get started by considering some everyday challenges faced by practitioners, and how prevention can be of help.

The Importance of Prevention to
Mental Health and Education Practitioners _____

The School Counselor

The alarm goes off—5:15 a.m. Time to move into the new week. Monday morning, and in a little more than two hours the sign on the door will say "the counselor is in" and the parade will begin. Teachers whose patience has been pushed to the limit by students not showing up on time, or at all. Parents crying for help because they are unable to exert influence on their children's lives. The gang wannabes who have already been tossed from class, and it is just the first day of the week. The kids with the rough weekend—too little supervision, too much access to grass. Students coming in for a termination interview—required to be an official "school leaver"—or dropout.

As a counselor, the goal is to help—but the wish is to roll over, turn off the alarm, and let someone else go in today to handle the incoming sea of sorrow brought each day by troubled students, teachers, and parents. There has to be a better way.

The Family Therapist

The years spent in training to be a family therapist, and it comes to this? Coming into the clinic, it is clear, the waiting room is already filled, and from the looks of the families, it will be a long and sorrowful day. You know the models of intervention, you know how to use paradox and circular and strategic questions, you know how to do family joining, and you know how to use rituals and family mapping and genograms. You understand triangulation and can facilitate detriangulation. But the families facing you today bring issues touched on, but not focused on, in the training program:

- *Unemployment:* not just losing a job, but losing everything, including the house, the car, and all that goes with it
- *Substance abuse:* not the type discussed in training where alcohol was a substitute for a less-than-fulfilling spousal relationship, but abuse that is the only thing keeping the parents going
- *Uncivilized children:* We aren't talking about mild oppositional defiant issues, or toilet training concerns, but about children who truly have not learned responsible social interactions, moral expectations, or just plain old "how to behave"—and you know what the future holds for them with schooling, community issues, and the likely juvenile court process.

Sufficient time will allow you to use your therapeutic skills, and yet you know you are likely to see the family only two or three times, the waiting room is full of others waiting their turn, and you are being expected to explain why you don't get better outcomes when using taxpayer dollars. There has to be a better way.

Practitioners in the fields of psychology, mental health, and education face the challenge of serving the needs of a very large population of people with mental, behavioral, and abuse problems. We understand why the problems exist, but the bottom line is that the prevalence of these problems is high, and we lack the resources and infrastructure to treat all affected individuals. The costs of treating these problems—and even more so, the costs of leaving them untreated—are burdensome to society and to individuals. We believe that prevention is a key component in addressing mental, behavioral, and abuse problems and reducing their costs and consequences.

The Prevalence of Mental, Behavioral, and Substance Use Disorders

A large number of people suffer from mental, behavioral, and abuse problems. A nationally representative evaluation of the lifetime prevalence and age of onset of anxiety, mood, impulse control, and substance use disorders found that nearly half of Americans will have at least one diagnosable disorder during their lifetime (Kessler, Berglund, et al., 2005). Approximately, 6 in 10 of these disorders will be considered serious or moderate (Kessler, Chiu, Demler, & Walters, 2005). Furthermore, the age of onset for these disorders is low; about half of all disorders begin by age 14, and 75% begin by age 24 (Kessler, Berglund, et al., 2005). Cross-national studies indicate that diagnosable mental, behavioral, and abuse disorders are common worldwide (WHO [World Health Organization] World Mental Health Survey Consortium, 2004).

Activity

What are the stats for your community? Do you know how many in your community live below the poverty level? How many drop out of school each year? How many are engaged in the juvenile court or youth detention services? How many rely on food stamps and other forms of aid to be able to sustain the family? How many are homeless, and what is the status of the homeless shelter services in your community?

Then, ask why? If there are very few in your community who are experiencing these issues, what is your community doing right to make this happen? If there are substantial numbers of people experiencing these concerns and issues, why? What would be contributing to the problem?

Then ask the tougher question: Could these issues be prevented and, if so, how? What steps would be necessary? Hopefully, by the time you have completed the *Prevention Practice Kit*, some clear directions, actions, and potential outcomes will be clear.

The Practical Limits of Treatment_____

Even in wealthy nations, the resources and infrastructure are not available to address every individual with mental, behavioral, or abuse problems. Therefore, these mental health issues often go untreated. Even in serious cases of mental disorder, 35.5% to 50.3% of people in developed countries received no treatment (WHO World Mental Health Survey Consortium, 2004). Within the United States, only 40% of people suffering from a recent mental, behavioral, or substance use disorder received treatment in the past year. Of those receiving mental health assistance, only one in three were classified by researchers as meeting a threshold for minimally adequate treatment (Wang et al., 2005). Our mental health and other support systems would need to grow substantially to meet the needs of all those suffering from mental, behavioral, and substance use problems; given current economic and political realities, it is unrealistic to expect such an expansion to occur. However, identifying these unmet mental health needs in the United States has prompted discussion on how we can more effectively allocate resources—such as through prevention—to reduce the human suffering and financial costs associated with these problems.

The Costs of Mental, Behavioral, and Substance Use Problems _____

Mental, behavioral, and substance use problems are enormously costly both to individuals and to society. The personal costs of these problems include mental anguish, financial hardship, strained relationships, and difficulty conducting day-to-day activities. Mental disorders have been found to adversely affect the ability to carry out normal activities more profoundly than many serious chronic physical illnesses, such as diabetes and arthritis (Kessler, Greenberg, Mickelson, Meneades, & Wang, 2001). A large international study found that the level of impairment (i.e., the number of days in the past year when the respondent was incapable of carrying out normal activities) was higher for respondents with even moderate mental health disorders than for respondents with severe chronic physical disorders (WHO World Mental Health Survey Consortium, 2004). This impairment may result in reduced educational and work-related opportunities, among other adverse consequences. Prevention efforts, especially those targeted at young people, may help stave off these negative outcomes and put individuals on a steadier path to well-being and success.

People who are close to the affected individual also bear the burdens of mental, behavioral, and substance use problems. Suffering from one or more of these problems may interfere with an individual's ability to maintain his or her role within a family, such as being an effective parent.

This impairment puts stress on relationships with the family—the relationship with the other parent and the relationship with the child. Alternately, the mental, behavioral, and substance use problems of a child will affect the lives of the parents and siblings (e.g., financial strain, increased experience of stress). Friendship networks and work relationships may be similarly affected. Our lives are interconnected; therefore, we expect that prevention efforts will take into account this connectedness. Successful prevention programs will result in benefits that extend beyond the affected individual in isolation.

Mental, behavioral, and substance use problems extract a heavy cost from communities and society. A large network of service providers and other systems, including mental health personnel, emergency rooms, criminal justice, child welfare, and educational systems, are called on to respond to these problems and their consequences. The promise of effective prevention includes societal benefits that can be readily measured (e.g., reduced costs of such services, less crime, higher productivity), along with those that are less quantifiable (e.g., increased overall well-being of the population).

Focusing for a moment on strictly the financial benefits, we see that if preventive efforts are able to produce even moderate reductions in the incidence of mental, behavioral, and substance use problems, the cost savings attained could be profound. For example, drug abuse cost society approximately $181 billion in 2002, including $107 billion in drug-related crime (National Institute on Drug Abuse, n.d.). Another study estimated the cost of mental, emotional, and behavioral disorders among young people at approximately $247 billion per year, including costs associated with health care, child welfare, education, juvenile justice, and criminal justice systems (Eisenberg & Neighbors, 2007). An examination of workplace costs of major depressive disorder estimated $36.6 billion per year in salary-equivalent lost productivity (Kessler et al., 2006).

The current state of the literature is somewhat limited with regard to research on cost-effectiveness and cost-benefits of preventive programs; however, this is an area of great promise, given positive findings thus far. See Book 8, *Public Policy and Mental Health*, in the *Prevention Practice Kit* for more on this topic. We expect to see in the future more evidence confirming that preventive interventions realize cost-savings with regard to long-term and short-term outcomes of mental, behavioral, and substance use problems.

A focus on prevention leads mental health and education practitioners to take an active role in warding off the negative consequences of mental, behavioral, and substance use problems, rather than solely being reactive to them. By way of analogy, compare the role of the gardener with the role of the mechanic. The mechanic is focused on fixing broken things. The gardener is concerned with creating and nurturing a thriving ecosystem. We argue that it is more fulfilling, creative, and impactful to be a gardener—that is, to help people thrive. Prevention helps people flourish. Given the widespread prevalence of mental, behavioral, and substance abuse problems, the costs and consequences of these problems, and our inability to treat all those who need help, prevention is vitally important.

Activity

At a conference luncheon of counselors, the person sitting on your right shares her view that "prevention is great when thinking about maintaining your car or your teeth, but it has no real value for mental health because it is undoable." You disagree and attempt to offer support for a preventive approach in mental health. Develop a one-page "statement" that contains the basic points of your argument and then try explaining it in a conversational way to a friend.

2

History and Present Status of Prevention

Challenges Remain

A s we consider the importance of prevention, it is also important to understand how it evolved over time. In doing so, we will discover that challenges remain to be solved in order for prevention to be fully integrated into training and practice in mental health today. Indeed, the history of prevention is an interesting one, full of starts and stops, and it exemplifies how a major approach builds iteratively over time.

Prevention is broadly interdisciplinary and depends on social–ecological contributions. Its theory, research, and applications—indeed, its very definition—have emerged through contributions from a variety of disciplines, including public health, psychology, social work, education, counseling, public policy, nursing, medicine, developmental ecology, environmental health, health promotion, physical therapy, occupational health, and more.

Due to the limited space available in this book, this section about the history and status of prevention will be centered on just one discipline and profession in prevention's panorama—counseling psychology. In many ways, it can serve as an illustration of prevention's evolution in the broader mental health and educational field. The account is adapted from a larger exposition on this general topic (Conyne, 2012).

Illustrations of Early Events

Prevention in counseling psychology emerged from developments in the multidisciplinary focus referred to as "prevention" and in relation to a set of themes in counseling psychology emphasizing strengths, person–environment fit, and social change.

Origins of counseling psychology (and its "cousin" profession, counseling/ counselor education) were tied to the educational, social organizing, and mental hygiene innovations of Jesse B. Davis, Frank Parsons (1909), and

Clifford Beers (1908). Their early contributions set the foundation, being guided by attention to themes revolving around prevention, as well as treatment.

The seeds for prevention were sown by Dr. John Snow. In 1854, during a raging cholera epidemic in London, Snow traced the source of water being consumed by residents and found that those drinking water from one of those lines experienced unusually high rates of cholera. His simple but highly effective experimental intervention was to remove the handle from the Broad Street water pump, thus denying polluted drinking water to users along that line. This environmental intervention, which was not conducted in a parallel water line, resulted in a noticeable plummeting in the incidence (rate of development of new cases) of cholera only among residents formerly served by water from the Broad Street pump. This public health strategy (remove the source of disease) became a bedrock principle of prevention.

Gerald Caplan built on environmental change and other public health principles to initially shape prevention in mental health. His conception of a three-tiered approach (Caplan, 1964), involving primary (i.e., before the appearance of a disorder), secondary (i.e., early in a disorder's progression), and tertiary prevention (i.e., repairing and restoring positive functioning) significantly altered understandings of mental health practice. After-the-fact treatment of existing psychological and emotional problems now could be understood as one approach instead of the only approach.

Dynamic Activity During the 1960s

The 1960s were a decade of disruption and dynamic change. The Vietnam War stimulated significant reactions both at home and abroad, including both peaceful and violent protests and demonstrations. Public discourse and demonstrations frequently occurred, leading to concerted activity in the areas of civil and women's rights and to young people's urgings for freedom and individual expression. Political assassinations cruelly cut short the lives of President John F. Kennedy, Senator Robert M. Kennedy, and Dr. Martin Luther King Jr. The "Great Society" of President Lyndon B. Johnson was introduced, as was the Community Mental Health Centers Act (noted for its mandate for preventive services), and Medicare and Medicaid. These initiatives, along with the Social Security Act decades earlier (1935), represented political strategies aimed at improving the economic and health status of Americans—including mental health.

Prevention Gains Strength in the 1970s

During the late 1960s and throughout the ensuing decade, prevention in mental health entered the professional practice and research arena, alongside the flourishing human potential movement. Notable accomplishments occurred in scholarly works and in political legislation.

Among the significant scholarly works that appeared were Caplan's (1964) identification of a tripartite conception of prevention, defined as primary, secondary, and tertiary prevention in his *Principles of Preventive Psychiatry*. His illustration of how mental health consultation could exert preventive effects was elaborated in the *Theory and Practice of Mental Health Consultation* (1970). Julian Rappaport's influential text on community psychology featuring prevention in a central role appeared in 1977, as did Klein and Goldston's (1977) compilation of papers endorsing primary prevention as an "idea whose time has come." (*Note:* Klein and Goldston turned out to be premature in their pronouncement.) The Vermont Conference on the Primary Prevention of Psychopathology began a series of meetings in 1975 that proved to be consequential in promoting research, scholarship, and practice in prevention. The end of the decade marked the publication of the first in a continuing series of influential national reports on the nation's health by the U.S. Surgeon General, *Healthy People: The Surgeon General's Report on Health Promotion and Disease Prevention* (1979); this volume was followed by updates in 1990, 2000, 2010, with 2020 being prepared.

Mental health and prevention garnered political attention, also, during this time. In 1973, the Health Maintenance Organization Act was passed, giving rise to the appearance of health maintenance organizations (HMOs) and the promise, yet to be realized, of supporting preventive mental health. Toward the end of the decade, President Carter established the President's Commission of Mental Health, which contained a Task Force on Prevention. At the highest political levels, prevention was gaining ground and beginning to exert a national impact.

Within counseling psychology, by the end of the 1960s, Jordaan, Myers, Layton, and Morgan (1968, cited in Whiteley, 1980, pp. 179–195) addressed the issue of roles for counseling psychologists inclusively. They defined three roles: (1) remedial, (2) developmental, and (3) *preventive*. "Prevention" now had entered the counseling psychology lexicon. Others, such as Clack (1975, cited in Whiteley, 1980, p. 201), Haskell (1975, pp. 201–202), and Ivey (1976, cited in Whiteley, 1980, pp. 196–204) began to define prevention as being proactive with a focus on skill development and environmental change.

A few innovative and risk-taking college and university counseling/student development centers (notably the first of these, established at Colorado State University, followed by Illinois State University and a handful of others) during this decade experimented with offering an array of campus-based preventive interventions, directions that largely went against typical practice then. These unique college and university counseling centers sought to augment the traditional remedially focused, individual-level delivery of service to students with developmental and preventive ones, aimed at students to be sure but also at other campus populations and at the campus environment itself. These offerings included environmental assessment and change programs, the use of trained student paraprofessionals, psychoeducation services, outreach programs to residence halls, an expanded repertoire of groups, institutional research, and preventive consultation with campus administrators and faculty members. These ongoing experiments also produced a body of literature supporting and describing them (e.g., Banning & Kaiser, 1974; Blocher, 1974; Conyne, 1975, 1978; Daher, Corazzini, & McKinnon, 1977; Ivey, 1976; Western Interstate Commission for Higher Education, 1972).

This comprehensive array of services reflected the culture of the times that emphasized change and experimentation. One of the seminal scholarly products that emerged was the publication of the "Counseling Intervention Cube" (Morrill, Oetting, & Hurst, 1974). This conceptual model clearly articulated remedial, developmental, and preventive goals for counseling interventions targeted at individual, group, and institutional levels that could be delivered directly or indirectly, including use of media. This document played a significant role in the evolution of counseling and counseling psychology because of the comprehensive schema posited for conceptualizing, designing, and evaluating a broad array of counseling interventions and the prominent place it accorded to those interventions intended to be preventive in their goals. Moreover, this document legitimized and gave impetus to the creative exploration of counseling psychology practice over decades. Two of the many sources appearing around this time included Drum and Figler's (1973) *Outreach in Counseling: Applying the Growth and Development Model in Schools and Colleges* and Judith and Michael Lewis's (1977, 1983) essential text *Community Counseling: A Human Services Approach* (which later expanded to Lewis, Lewis, Daniels, & D'Andrea's *Community Counseling: Empowerment Strategies for a Diverse Society*, first published in 2003).

At the beginning of the next decade, Whiteley (1980) edited a legacy volume summarizing critical developmental points in the origins and growth of counseling psychology from the early 1900s. Suggestive hints and some support for prevention run throughout this period, but it was not until the 1970s that prevention in counseling psychology received direct attention and support, however, ambivalently and inconsistently.

Prevention Broadens From the 1980s to 2010

1980 to 1989

The work of Albee was of central importance. Among other contributions, he pointed out that preventive interventions in mental health are the only way to reduce the incidence of a disorder (i.e., the number of new cases or the rate of development of any disorder) and that all other approaches, no matter how vitally important, were able to make only "after-the-fact" adjustments. He defined incidence reduction as employing a strengths/stressors ratio, thereby providing a means for prevention program design and evaluation to proceed intentionally (Albee, 1982, 1985). A second especially significant contribution made by Albee was to closely connect prevention with social justice and system change (Albee, 1986). He believed that social pathogens were at the root of mental health problems and that these unhealthy conditions were located most frequently and intensely in poor communities. Eradicating poverty and other forms of social and economic inequity from these communities—and from society in general—is a preventive strategy of high priority, he urged.

Rappaport, who had authored an already important text in community psychology (1977) suggested in his Presidential Address to the Division of Community Psychology (Rappaport, 1981) that empowerment is an essential process for any prevention effort, and collaborative participation afforded a key strategy. He insisted that preventionists should be careful to work *with* people not do things *to* them in projects that should aim toward promoting increased control by program participants over decisions and power in a community.

Through a series of insightful publications, Cowen expanded and deepened the understanding of preventive mental health. Cowen's (1980, 1983, 1985, & 2000) discussions of person-centered preventive approaches were especially instrumental. Not to be confused with the person-centered counseling of Carl Rogers, Cowen indicated that person-centered prevention strategies could proceed through two routes by helping people (1) anticipate and cope more positively with the stressful life situations they face, such as divorce; and (2) enhance their life competency skills through skill training, being involved in competency-facilitating experiences, such as mentoring, and learning how to positively alter the major settings of their lives, such as school, work, and family.

Gordon (1983) developed an influential and unique conception of prevention. It was later elaborated by Mrazek and Haggerty (1994) and then adopted by the prestigious Institute of Medicine. This schema contrasted with the tripartite concept of primary, secondary, and tertiary prevention yet still envisioned three types: (1) "universal," addressing an entire population; (2) "selective," addressing a subset of a population deemed to be at potential risk; and (3) "indicated," addressing another subset of a population deemed to be at clear risk.

An important prevention publication appearing within counselor education and counseling psychology during this time was the double issue of the *Personnel and Guidance Journal* coedited by Shaw and Goodyear (1984), "Primary Prevention in Schools," and Goodyear and Shaw (1984), "Primary Prevention on Campus and in the Community." These collections of articles demonstrated that preventive interventions were a reality throughout the educational system of the United States. At the same time, a published survey of counseling psychology training programs (McNeil & Ingram, 1983) documented the relative absence of prevention training.

Conyne's (1987) text, *Primary Preventive Counseling: Empowering People and Systems*, followed 3 years later. When written, Conyne thought that prevention within counseling psychology and counselor education was on the precipice of emerging strongly as a force; the fact that it took another 17 years for the second edition of this book to appear was one indication that a longer-range perspective was needed.

Also in 1987, the Third National Conference of Counseling Psychology, known as the "Georgia Conference" (University of Georgia), met to define the future of counseling psychology. Along with asserting the importance of traditional approaches, such as individual therapy, considerable attention was given to proactive outreach and to working with diverse populations and emerging settings. Prevention, life-span development, skill building, and other "innovative and nontraditional functions" emerged among the themes of the Conference, giving credence to their future viability.

Price, Cowen, Lorion, and Ramos-McKay (1988) edited an American Psychological Association (APA)-sponsored publication, *14 Ounces of Prevention: A Casebook for Practitioners*, culminating an intense, judged project to identify excellent prevention programs. Fourteen exemplary prevention programs occurring across the life span were selected from a thorough review of 300 submitted program proposals. Detailed descriptions of these effective prevention programs were intended to provide concrete guidance to benefit practice, teaching, and research. As a whole, these positively evaluated programs demonstrated that prevention could be delivered through carefully created, delivered, and monitored programs. The detailed methodologies for each program provided readers with unusually explicit information about design and implementation approaches.

1990 to 1999

Designing and conducting prevention programs systematically and scientifically was addressed by Coie and his associates (1993) in the document, "The Science of Prevention." A national research agenda for prevention was suggested. This document presented a cogent argument for developing an evidence base for prevention, which has become an ongoing initiative in mental health and in preventive mental health.

For instance, Tobler published a number of studies, including meta-analyses (e.g., Tobler, 1993; Tobler & Stratton, 1997) investigating the effectiveness of substance abuse prevention programs. Durlak and Wells (1997) published a large meta-analysis of 177 prevention programs demonstrating that these programs produced 59% to 82% significantly more positive outcomes than were realized by control group participants In another large study, Nation et al. (2003) used a review-of-reviews approach to identify principles of prevention programs found to be effective. These principles include comprehensiveness, use of varied teaching methods, containing sufficient dosage, being theory driven, delivered with appropriate timing, being socioculturally relevant, possessing outcome evaluation, and using well-trained staff.

In 1996, the Center for the Study and Prevention of Violence (CSPV) at the University of Colorado at Boulder launched its "Blueprints for Violence Prevention" project. Employing sets of selection criteria, "model" and "promising" prevention programs—called "Blueprints"—were identified that have demonstrated effectiveness. The resulting online resource (http://www.colorado.edu/cspv/blueprints/) is easily accessible and provides researchers and program developers with useful guidance about prevention programs that work.

While evidence mounts for the effectiveness of prevention, the archival definition of counseling psychology (APA, 1999), which still is currently in place, does little more than hint at a place for prevention: "Psychoeducational/preventive programming" is identified as a procedure and technique for counseling psychology, which the statement indicates can be "preventive, skill enhancing, or remedial." This condition is not unique to counseling psychology but, rather, tends to characterize general mental health training and practice.

Although some exceptions exist, counseling psychology and counselor education curricula generally remain to be penetrated by either specialized courses in prevention or by courses in which prevention is infused (Conyne, Newmeyer, Kenny, Romano, & Matthews, 2008; Matthews, 2003, 2004). Hage and Romano (2010) drew from the 2009 APA Presidential Task Force on the Future of Psychology Practice, which noted that psychologists need expanded models of training to prepare them for "the new world psychology finds itself in" (Martin, 2009, p. 67). Certainly, expanded training in prevention is one such area for future development, yet multiple academic priorities continue to vie for attention and inclusion. Prevention training—while endorsed—too often fails to be elevated to course or concentration status.

Yet a third large gap needs to be closed, in addition to curricula and research, and that is advocating that prevention becomes a core part of roles, functions, tasks, and positions that are assumed by counseling psychologists. As Hage and Romano (2010) observe, work involvement of counseling psychologists in prevention seems to be decreasing over time (Fretz & Simon, 1992; Goodyear et al., 2008). For substantiation, they point to a random sample survey of counseling psychologists, reporting that only about one quarter of those responding ($n = 167$) engage in prevention/outreach activities (Goodyear et al., 2008). This figure can be compared with more than one third ($n = 232$, 35.9%) of counseling psychologists who reported participating in primary prevention activities 15 years earlier (Watkins, Lopez, Campbell, & Himmel, 1986). The apparent downward slope of prevention activity contrasts with an increasing level of attention being given to it, as measured by the quantity of scholarly production that has been accelerating since around 1980 and to larger political initiatives and legislation that has occurred over the decades. Clearly, attention needs to be given to how counseling psychologists and those from other helping professions can deliver prevention in their work and to get properly paid for it. Health care reform may help spur and focus energies to this end.

2000 to 2012

Romano and Hage (2000c), Conyne (2000), and Britner and O'Neil (2008) have issued "calls for action" to resolve and strengthen the place of prevention in counseling psychology. As Romano and Hage (2000b) put it with regard to the archival definition of counseling psychology, there is a need to

> modify the archival definition of counseling psychology . . . to clearly state prevention as a fundamental activity of the profession. In the current definition, prevention is suggested; it is time for prevention to be unambiguously identified as central to counseling psychology. (p. 855)

During the new millennium, attention to "positive mental health" gained renewed impetus from a variety of areas, including positive psychology, health promotion, health psychology, strength-based psychology, wellness, life skills, resilience, social justice, advocacy, stress reduction, coping, and aspects of neuropsychology. In addition, a number of publications addressed "system change" as a medium for promoting health, noticeably in the areas of social justice, multicultural counseling, and advocacy. Because both positive mental health and system change are fundamental elements of prevention, it seems ironic that prevention has not been included centrally within discussions of these concepts and approaches (the Kenny, Horne, Orpinas, & Reese, 2009, resource on social justice and preventive interventions is a clear exception). One wonders, therefore, "Where is prevention in these positive mental health and system change approaches?"

Conversely, it is encouraging to find that attention to prevention in counseling psychology accelerated during the 2000s, although a review of scholarly activity in prevention published in counseling journals by O'Byrne, Brammer, Davidson, and Poston (2002) revealed "a relative paucity" of volume (p. 330). Still, gains were occurring. The 2008 edition of Brown and Lent's *Handbook of Counseling Psychology* reached out, however modestly, to include prevention by giving it at least some tangential coverage, a gain not realized in previous editions. Recent summaries of prevention history compiled by Kenny and Romano (2009) and by Hage and Romano (2010) document the increasing pace of prevention activity and its recognition. Another clear marker of this progression was the formal establishment of the Prevention Section in 2000 within the Society of Counseling Psychology, after years of incremental advancement.

According to its Bylaws (2006), the purpose of the Prevention Section is to further the theory, research, teaching, and practice of prevention, advocacy, and public interest initiatives among counseling psychologists. The Section describes itself as incorporating a full array of preventive, developmental, policy, advocacy, and community-focused activities. Specific objectives of this Section, which mirror those of the Prevention and Public Interest Special Interest Group (SIG) from which it came are to (a) bring together counseling psychologists who have an interest in prevention through their teaching, practice, and/or research activities (the networking may occur through newsletters, convention programs, and/or individual communications); (b) promote the practice and research of prevention within counseling psychology; (c) facilitate communication between counseling psychology and other groups within APA, including APA's Public Interest Directorate and the Board for the Advancement of Psychology in the Public Interest (BAPPI); and (d) give visibility to the teaching, practice, and research initiatives of counseling psychologists in their prevention, advocacy, and public policy activities.

At about the same time the Prevention Section was being formed, Romano and Hage's (2000a) major contribution in *The Counseling Psychologist*, "Prevention in Counseling Psychology," appeared, representing an important milestone in counseling psychology. Among other notable features, it presented an integrative definition of prevention that included five dimensions (stop, delay, reduce, strengthen, and support) and set forth four major agenda for advancing prevention in counseling psychology: (1) increased use of integrative and systemic models and approaches, (2) greater emphasis on early preventive interventions with children and youth, (3) integrating preventive interventions with diversity, and (4) advancing training through attention to eight domains and sets of related skills that support the science and practice of prevention. That publication deserves much credit for nurturing and stimulating much of the prevention energy and output being witnessed in the Society of Counseling Psychology over the past decade.

The topic of "prevention groups" received considerable attention during this time period, initiated by the document, "Recommendations of the APA Division Task Force for the Use of Groups for Prevention" (2000). Two special issues of group-oriented journals (in counseling and in psychology) focused on groups being used to accomplish prevention goals: (1) The *Journal for Specialists in Group Work* (Conyne & Horne, 2001) addressed "The Use of Groups for Prevention" and (2) *Group Dynamics: Theory, Research, and Practice* (Conyne & Clanton Harpine, 2010) published "Prevention Groups: Evidence-Based Approaches to Advance the Field." Other publications focused on prevention groups included those by Conyne (2004a), Conyne and Hage (2009), Hage and Romano (2010), Waldo, Schwartz, Horne, and Cote (2011), and in the Social Work discipline, a chapter by Nash and Snyder (2004). See Book 4 in this *Kit* on *Prevention Groups* by Clanton Harpine.

In 2001, the Fourth National Counseling Psychology Conference in Houston advanced social justice, innovative approaches, and advocacy for the profession and for underserved populations. *The Handbook for Social Justice in Counseling Psychology* (Toporek, Gerstein, Fouad, Roysicar, & Israel, 2006) was one important example of the generativity spawned by that Conference. The *Handbook's* introductory chapter, "Social Justice and Counseling Psychology in Context" (Fouad, Gerstein, & Toporek, 2006), provides a compelling rationale for their interconnection. Rattling around in all this exciting work is prevention—but one has to look fairly hard to find it. The Houston Conference was followed 7 years later by the Chicago Conference, where counseling psychologists were asked to consider and advance their work in international and global affairs.

Enough scholarly work in prevention, however, had accumulated to easily support the compilation in 2003 of Gullotta and Bloom's edited volume, *Encyclopedia of Primary Prevention and Health Promotion*. This comprehensive product, organized from a social work perspective, demonstrates the breadth and depth of prevention practice and research and also serves to remind us that prevention is a multidisciplinary approach that both derives from and transcends several sources. Durlak's (2003) chapter on effective prevention and mental health programming was notable for its suggestions on the topic.

The prevention guidelines (Hage et al., 2007) referred to earlier were published in what was to become an award-winning article in *The Counseling Psychologist*. They contain suggestions for counseling psychologists about prevention practice, education, and research. In 2008, a work group of Prevention Section members began reshaping the article's contents into the prescribed pattern for formally approved Guidelines that is stipulated by APA Governance. Benefitting from procedural consultation provided and initial review of its work by relevant APA committees, the final document, currently with the title, *Guidelines for Prevention Practice, Research, and Education*, was submitted by the Prevention Section work group to APA Governance in February, 2010 and has been proceeding through rounds of review. Final action awaits as this document was finalized in June of 2012.

A series of prevention in counseling psychology volumes was published during the last half of the decade, beginning with the second edition of Conyne's *Preventive Counseling* (2004b). A series of social justice–prevention sources also appeared, attesting to the growing importance of this linkage. Reese and Vera (2007) published a major contribution in *The Counseling Psychologist* on "Culturally Relevant Prevention," as did Herman and associates (2007) on "Culturally Sensitive Health Care and Counseling Psychology." Other important social justice and prevention resources include chapters by Vera and Spreight (2003), Spreight and Vera (2008), and by Vera, Buhim, and Isacco (2009); Toporek et al.'s (2006) *Handbook for Social Justice in Counseling Psychology*; and Kenny, et al.'s (2009) edited work, *Realizing*

Social Justice: The Challenge of Preventive Interventions. The Preface to that book by the coeditors and its initial chapter (Kenny & Romano, 2009) clearly project the positive correlation between social justice and prevention.

Positive psychology, along with social justice, represents a scholarly and practice domain connected closely to both counseling psychology and prevention. A number of publications in the area of positive psychology emerged during this period, as well. Examples include Seligman's *Authentic Happiness* (2002a) and two edited volumes by Snyder and Lopez, their *Handbook of Positive Psychology* (2002) and *Positive Psychology: The Scientific and Practical Explorations of Human Strengths* (2007). Connections of positive psychology with both counseling psychology (Lopez & Edwards, 2008; Lopez et al., 2006; Smith, 2006) and prevention (e.g., Conyne, 2004a; Seligman, 2002b) have been highlighted, yet await significantly fuller development. Conyne's (2010) book on program development and evaluation processes applied to prevention demonstrates the reliance of prevention programming on planning and evaluation processes.

3

Definitions of Prevention

As its history unfolded, understandings of just what prevention *is* became clearer. Prevention, as defined and used in everyday language, is a relatively straightforward concept. The *Oxford English Dictionary* (2011, online version) defines prevention as "the action of keeping from happening or making impossible an anticipated event or intended act." This definition is widely understood, and it reflects the way the word is used in general discussion about the prevention of high school dropout, cavities, or the spread of the flu, for example. However, to experts immersed in these fields, prevention may be defined in somewhat different ways. Before we lay out some of these definitions of prevention, let's take a moment to examine each of these examples in a little more detail.

How do we stop the spread of the flu? We first need to consider the chain of events that leads to a person becoming ill. There must be exposure to the virus, and the virus must be able to take hold in the person's body. Prevention efforts aim to interrupt this chain. Some efforts endeavor to limit exposure, such as through regular hand washing, covering sneezes, and avoiding others who are sick. Other efforts, such as flu shots, reduce the risk of infection if you are exposed.

Prevention efforts often involve different levels of activity targeted toward populations at varying levels of vulnerability. In the case of the flu, public health officials aim some messages at the public at large, while subpopulations receive additional attention. For example, flu shots are recommended for everyone, but public health workers may expend extra effort to reach vulnerable populations (e.g., pregnant women, older adults).

Preventing cavities is also a concern of public health workers, but this example is different from the flu because cavities are not spread from person to person. However, there is still a chain of events that leads to the development of cavities, and the goal is still to stop this progression. Some populations are more at risk for developing cavities (e.g., young people) and more focus is placed on them. Although young people may be more susceptible to cavities, the factors contributing to the development of cavities go beyond just the behavior of this population. For example, the attitudes and behaviors of parents will affect whether children develop cavities. If parents regularly provide their toddler with sippy cups of soda, what is the best way to change this harmful behavior? The preventionist must consider the cultural, environmental, and economic factors (e.g., soda may be cheaper than milk; many believe it tastes better than water) that contribute to the behavior in the first place. These considerations must be coupled with an understanding of the types of information and supports that will make positive change more likely.

A related example expands on the idea that even a seemingly straightforward problem—preventing cavities—may become quite complex. The use of stimulant drugs such as methamphetamines is related to the development of cavities. Methamphetamines can decimate a mouth full of healthy teeth, but it is likely that most dentists know little about how to prevent meth addiction. Efforts to prevent meth addiction are more likely to incidentally prevent cavities than efforts to prevent cavities are likely to prevent meth addiction. However, as more dentists face the impact of drug abuse on their patients, they will likely become more engaged in efforts to prevent addiction.

Now we will shift away from the field of public heath to an issue of more concern to psychologists, educators, social workers, and counselors. In trying to prevent high school dropout, the goal is to interrupt the process that leads to quitting school. But what causes a student to drop out? The causes may be different for different students, and for each individual, there may be one big reason (e.g., academic failure, drug addiction) or many small reasons (e.g., poor grades, financial hardship at home, boredom). In the case where many interconnected and overlapping factors contribute to the development of a problem, prevention efforts can be successful, but they are also more complex. Along with this complexity comes the need for experts in different fields to shed light on various aspects of the problem. Dropout prevention efforts must consider academic, social, cultural, and economic contributors, among others, that influence student behavior. It is unlikely that one researcher would have expertise in all of these fields. Therefore, effective prevention is a multidisciplinary endeavor.

It is also impossible to prevent dropout in a vacuum. In other words, to successfully prevent dropout, you will have to ameliorate other problems—for example, drug use, delinquency, academic failure, economic strain—as well. Especially in the field of education and mental health, problems have multiple causes, and these causes are associated with multiple negative effects. The good news is that by addressing these causes early, we have the potential to prevent a large swath of related outcomes. For example, if we are able to increase literacy in elementary school, we will affect a host of outcomes in high school and beyond (e.g., reduced dropout, increased employment opportunities).

This discussion has aimed to highlight several important concepts regarding prevention:

- Prevention is a multidisciplinary field, impacting and engaging with medicine, public health, psychology, counseling, education, social work, among others.
- Because prevention is used in many different fields, it has been defined and classified in different ways over time. We will present the most influential definitions next.
- Successful prevention requires a big picture perspective. Connections between experts in many different fields are crucial to understand and prevent problems.
- It is often difficult to narrowly focus on one prevention goal, especially in the psychology and education fields. Problems in these areas tend to have multiple causes. By addressing these causes, we may be able to prevent a wide range of negative outcomes.

Now that we have gotten a flavor for the interconnected and interdisciplinary nature of prevention, let's take a look at the ways in which prevention has been defined and categorized through time.

Some common questions that have driven these definitions and classification schemes are as follows:

- At what populations are prevention efforts targeted?
- How is prevention different from treatment? From health promotion?

In this section, we review two classification systems that have been important in the history of prevention. Then we discuss some of the modern perspectives that shape conversations about prevention today.

Caplan's Classification: Primary, Secondary, and Tertiary Prevention

Caplan (1964) proposed a three-pronged classification scheme for categorizing types of prevention efforts within the mental health field. This classification scheme is based on a public health perspective. Caplan translated the ideas of primary, secondary, and tertiary prevention (already in use in public health) into the practice of prevention in the mental health field. Informed by public health, Caplan emphasized the community focus of prevention; the focus of prevention is on reducing and counteracting illness *at the community level*.

Primary prevention is concerned with preventing new cases of disorder (i.e., in public health terminology, reducing incidence). Primary prevention "involves lowering the rate of new cases of mental disorder in a population over a certain period by counteracting harmful circumstances before they have had a chance to produce illness" (Caplan, 1964, p. 26). This definition is similar to the common usage of prevention (i.e., as defined above in the *Oxford English Dictionary*), as it emphasizes stopping an unwanted event from happening. An example from mental health of primary prevention is taking action to prevent new cases of depression from occurring, such as through efforts to increase social connectedness among community members who may otherwise be isolated, or by addressing financial circumstances that can contribute to depression.

Secondary prevention involves lowering the rate of existing cases of mental disorder (i.e., reducing prevalence) by shortening the duration of illness through early diagnosis and remediation. This area of prevention extends beyond stopping something from happening, and thus goes beyond the familiar definition of prevention. An example of secondary prevention is screening efforts to identify people who are experiencing depression but have not yet sought treatment. Through early identification and intervention, the overall impact of the illness on society may be lessened.

Tertiary prevention is concerned with reducing the debilitating consequences of existing illness at the community level. For example, tertiary prevention may involve efforts to help people who are experiencing (or have just recovered from) depression to "return to their productive capacity as quickly as possible" (Caplan, 1964, p. 113). Caplan stresses that tertiary prevention encompasses community-level efforts rather than actions aimed individually, which he deems "rehabilitation." Tertiary prevention may include structural aspects such as adequate access to follow-up treatment or cultural aspects such as reducing the stigma of mental illness, which may interfere with the ability of individuals who have experienced mental illness to lead productive lives.

While Caplan's model is still influential, it has come under some criticism and is not the current prevailing model for the prevention of mental health problems. Caplan's classification scheme involves efforts that take place before, during, and after an illness or problem has occurred. For some critics, this overextends the reach of prevention into the realm of treatment (e.g., Baker & Shaw, 1987). Furthermore, Romano and Hage (2000a) argue that it may be difficult to differentiate between primary, secondary, and tertiary prevention efforts in the field of mental health due to the complex etiology and interconnected nature of mental health problems.

Gordon's Classification: Universal, Selective, Indicated

Gordon (1987) provided a conceptualization of types of prevention that focuses on the characteristics of the intended audience. This classification system defines three levels of prevention based on a risk–benefit balance that considers the risk of the disorder along with the costs of the prevention effort. Typically, as efforts become more intensive, they also become more costly both in terms of the resources needed to carry out the intervention and the amount of time and effort required by participants. Therefore, more intensive interventions may only be appropriate for individuals at elevated risk.

Three levels of prevention presented by Gordon are universal, selective, and indicated. Universal prevention involves measures that would benefit the entire population regardless of their level of risk for developing the targeted disorder or problem. For example, a primary prevention intervention focused on high school dropout may provide information for all students regarding graduation requirements. Selective prevention efforts are aimed at individuals with elevated risk. These efforts are typically more intensive, such as individual academic advising sessions for students who have gotten off track to graduate. Indicated preventions target those at high risk. Indicated preventions may include implementing an intensive, multipronged plan to address a failing student's needs and make graduation attainable.

An Example of the Universal/Indicated Model: The Multisite Violence Prevention Program

The Multisite Violence Prevention Project is an example of an intervention that provided differentiated levels of prevention. The Multisite Violence Prevention Project is also known as the GREAT Schools and Families Program (Guiding Responsibility and Expectations in Adolescents Today and Tomorrow). This large-scale, randomized clinical trial study was funded by the Centers for Disease Control and Prevention (CDC) to examine the effectiveness of different levels of preventive interventions for addressing aggression and bullying in schools. The program was a collaboration between the CDC and four universities: the University of Georgia, Virginia Commonwealth University, Duke University, and the University of Illinois at Chicago Medical School.

The GREAT Schools and Families Program was implemented in 37 middle schools, with 8 to 12 schools participating per site. Each school was randomly assigned to one of four conditions: universal, indicated, combined universal/indicated, and control (Miller-Johnson, Sullivan, Simon, & the Multisite Violence Prevention Project, 2004). The prevention goal of the study was to reduce overall levels of bullying and aggression across the sixth-grade population. For a more complete description of the GREAT Schools and Families Program, including the study population and measures, see the special supplement to the *American Journal of Preventive Medicine*, Prevention of Youth Violence: The Multisite Violence Prevention Project (Ikeda et al., 2004).

The Universal Condition. Approximately one fourth of all schools were randomly assigned to the universal condition. Schools assigned to the universal condition received preventive interventions broadly aimed at all sixth-grade students and teachers. The teacher component consisted of an initial 12-hour workshop and 10 weekly support group sessions. The goals of the teacher program were to (a) develop awareness and understanding of the problem of bullying, including risk and protective factors; (b) increase the use of effective strategies to prevent aggression; (c) enhance classroom management skills; and (d) develop skills to help victims of bullying. The teacher training and support group sessions were led by trained project staff, and the curriculum materials were manualized to encourage consistency across schools and sites (Orpinas, Horne, & the Multisite Violence Prevention Project, 2004).

The following topics were covered in the initial teacher training:

Aggression in Schools: What Is Happening?

    Examining the magnitude of the problem

    Defining types of violence

    Recognizing the bully, victim, bystander

    Analyzing students' risk and protective factors

Reflections: Developing Long-Term Goals

    Assessing and prioritizing classroom goals

    Applying a solution-focused approach

    Analyzing personal characteristics that influence class management

    Examining personal needs for emotional and physical well-being (e.g., stress management and support)

Setting Up for Success: Preventive Approach to Reducing Aggression

    Examining personal teaching styles: from control to cooperation

    Strengthening a positive relationship with students: communication patterns

    Establishing a positive and respectful classroom environment

    Enhancing successful strategies for classroom management and procedures (e.g., rules and routines, rewards and punishment, effective discipline)

Management of Power Struggles and Aggression

    Applying effective strategies for

        Resolving conflicts

        Defusing conflicts

        Dealing with disruptive students

        Reporting conflict

    Responding to crisis situations

    Assisting the targets of violence

Throughout the workshop, core values of the program were discussed: (a) a positive relationship between teachers and students is crucial to a successful classroom, (b) everyone in the school deserves to be treated with dignity and respect, and (c) bullying and aggression are not acceptable (Orpinas et al., 2004).

The teacher component also included weekly teacher support groups to help maintain positive changes over time. These meetings, led by trained project staff, offered teachers the opportunity to revisit and reinforce the topics covered in the initial training through activities and discussion. Specifically, teachers shared the real-life situations they were dealing with in their classrooms and received support and guidance from the group. Project staff and other teacher-participants served as a resource for brainstorming problems and generating solutions to prevent bullying and enhance classroom climate (Orpinas et al., 2004).

The student portion of the universal prevention intervention consisted of twenty 40-minute lessons implemented weekly in all sixth-grade classrooms in the school by trained staff facilitators. The goals of the student component were to (a) demonstrate positive problem-solving skills, (b) increase self-efficacy and motivation for using those skills, (c) foster positive school norms, and (d) reduce school norms supportive of aggression. Each lesson covered a topic relevant to preventing bullying, including the following:

Application of a Problem-Solving Model—SCIDDLE

> Stop
>
> Calm down
>
> Identify the problem and your feelings
>
> Decide among your options
>
> Do it
>
> Look back
>
> Evaluate

GREAT Choices for Now (i.e., skills for addressing conflict in the short term)

> Avoid
>
> Ignore
>
> Ask for help

GREAT Choices for Life (i.e., skills for addressing conflict in the long term)

> Getting along with others
>
> Demonstrating respect and dignity
>
> Turning down the heat (i.e., diffusing tension)
>
> Talking it out (i.e., communication skills)
>
> Being a helper

The curriculum is highly interactive, including small group activities and experiential learning. Each lesson builds cumulatively on the topics and ideas presented earlier in the curriculum. Training and curriculum materials were manualized to support consistency in implementation across sites (Meyer, Allison, Reese, Gay, & the Multisite Violence Prevention Project, 2004).

The Indicated Condition. While the universal program aimed to reach all sixth-grade students and teachers in the school, the indicated prevention selectively aimed prevention efforts at a small subset of high-risk students and their families. The indicated prevention consisted of 15 weekly family group sessions of approximately 2 hours each. The sessions, led by trained project staff, included approximately four to six families per group, and all family members (e.g., parents, caretakers, siblings) were invited to participate in the meetings. Students were targeted for inclusion in the program based on teacher ratings. Teachers identified the students who were considered high risk based on (a) an aggressive and disruptive pattern of behavior and (b) being influential among their peers. By reducing aggressive behaviors among this group of students, the prevention program aimed to reduce overall support and use of aggression among the entire sixth-grade population (Phillips Smith et al., 2004).

The family sessions included activities focused on the following:

Strengthening positive parenting practices, such as appropriate monitoring and supervision

Promoting care and respect through discipline and support

Increasing parent and child life-coping skills in managing behavior

Strengthening communication and problem-solving skills within the family

Promoting a strong family–school partnership and other networks of support

Planning for the future (i.e., developing academic and developmental goals for children)

The family program included discussion, activities, and homework focused on these goals. The format of the meetings included a review of the previous meeting and homework, a discussion of the current topic, role-playing and other activities, and closure/assignment of homework. The sessions allowed families the opportunity to learn and practice new skills, gain awareness of risk and protective factors, and foster social support among families who may be facing similar challenges. Furthermore, the interactive nature of the program was designed for families to learn from each other and share solutions that work in real-life circumstances.

Across all sites, family groups shared the same topics, activities, and homework for the 15 sessions (Phillips Smith et al., 2004).

The Combined Condition. Approximately one fourth of schools were randomly assigned to receive a combined intervention of the universal prevention program and the indicated prevention program. In these schools, the general population of sixth-grade students participated in the student curriculum, sixth-grade teachers participated in support groups, and family groups were targeted at students identified as more aggressive and influential than their peers. This research design allowed for the possibility of examining the impact of each intervention (i.e., universal, indicated) separately and in combination (Henry, Farrell, & the Multisite Violence Prevention Project, 2004).

The Control Condition. Approximately one fourth of schools were randomly assigned to receive no intervention. These schools served as a control group for comparison with schools in the other three conditions (Henry et al., 2004).

Outcomes of the Program. The results of the project are still being analyzed and reported, but several published papers describe results from different components of the program (e.g., The Multisite Violence Prevention Project, 2008, 2009). Overall, the pattern of findings has been complex (Multisite Violence Prevention Project, 2009). The evidence in support of the program includes the following:

- Relative to control schools, the general population of students in indicated intervention schools reported lower frequencies of self-reported physical aggression and teacher-reported aggression (Multisite Violence Prevention Project, 2009). These results indicate that a prevention program that is selectively aimed at a high-risk population can yield benefits for the broader population.
- Relative to control schools, students in universal intervention schools reported greater decreases in relational aggression over time. However, other outcomes related to reductions in aggression were not in the intended direction (Multisite Violence Prevention Project, 2009).
- Students with the highest levels of pre-intervention risk benefitted most from participating in the interventions. These students reported relatively lower levels of aggression at posttest than comparable students at control schools (Multisite Violence Prevention Project, 2009).
- Teachers who participated in the teacher program became more knowledgeable and confident in their skills and abilities to address bullying in their classrooms.

Furthermore, the extensive follow-up of students participating in the GREAT Schools and Families Program through high school at one university site has continued to yield important implications for prevention. For example, one set of studies identifies groups of students with similar profiles of risk and protective factors in sixth grade and compares these groups on measures of behavioral and academic outcomes in high school (Raczynski, Wetherington, Orpinas, & Horne, 2010; Wetherington, Raczynski, Orpinas, & Horne, 2010). A particular focus of this research is comparing the rate of dropout across groups of students with similar characteristics in sixth grade. By identifying distinct profiles of characteristics that are associated with problematic outcomes such as dropout, researchers may be able to develop more individualized prevention efforts. For example, students who are at potential risk for dropping out due to a deficit in academic skills may require a different type of support than students who are at risk for dropping out due to behavior problems. In this study, students in the universal condition did find benefit from the intervention, with all students in the schools being exposed to more effective problem-solving, decision-making, and conflict resolution skills, and with the students in the indicated treatment—the most aggressive—benefitting from the more intense, targeted, and behavior-focused interventions.

Activity

The phrase "Few, Some, All" is a simple way to remember the levels of Gordon's classification. That is, few people will need the intensive support at the indicated level, some people will need targeted intervention at the selective level, and all people will need basic skills and resources for positive living at the universal level. Given an area that is of interest to you, identify possible prevention activities that would benefit few, some, and all individuals.

Gordon's Classification Scheme Today

Gordon's classification scheme continues to enjoy widespread use. A high profile set of reports issued by the Institute of Medicine (1994; O'Connell, Boat, & Warner, 2009) advanced a classification scheme that included Gordon's three levels of prevention. The 2009 report outlined four approaches on a continuum of addressing mental health problems:

1. *Mental Health Promotion* refers to efforts to enhance well-being, including a sense of competence, positive self-esteem, social inclusion, and resiliency.

2. *Prevention* refers to efforts to prevent the onset of mental health problems at the universal, selective, and indicated levels.

3. *Treatment* refers to identifying individuals with mental health problems and providing standard remediation.

4. *Maintenance* refers to efforts to promote long-term adherence to treatment, with the goal of reduction of relapse. Furthermore, maintenance efforts include appropriate aftercare (i.e. rehabilitation).

Additional Perspectives on Prevention

While the universal, selective, and indicated classification scheme is popular and has been adopted by the Institute of Medicine, it is not the only conception of prevention in use. In this section, we consider other perspectives that have shaped the way that prevention is defined and practiced.

Prevention and Health Promotion

Prevention and health promotion are closely related. Cowen (1973) advanced health promotion as a second prong of prevention. Prevention efforts that include aspects of health promotion emphasize enhancing strengths and fostering well-being as well as reducing risk factors. The ultimate goal of health promotion is for individuals to lead healthy, thriving lives.

Many preventive efforts have emphasized a narrow risk reduction focus. In the field of public health, this model is generally appropriate. Think back to our earlier example; if our goal is to stop the spread of flu, it makes a lot of sense to focus our efforts on risk reduction, such as lowering potential exposure to the virus.

However, in the fields of mental health and education, an approach to prevention that only focuses on risk reduction doesn't take into account the complex and interconnected nature of the causes of problems. For instance, we cannot prevent child abuse in the absence of promoting healthy parenting. To stop parents from harming their children, the negative behavior needs to be replaced with adaptive behavior. Furthermore, the factors that influence the development of parenting behavior are not merely individual; cultural, environmental, economic, political, and societal factors influence and interact with individual characteristics to affect behavior, for better or worse. Prevention in the mental health and education fields cannot solely follow a disease-based model that is narrowly focused on reducing risk factors.

Prevention and Social Justice

The field of prevention has been influenced by a social justice perspective, especially the work of George Albee. Social, economic, and political conditions often serve to perpetuate inequity and attendant mental health problems. Therefore,

> A social justice vision of prevention . . . seeks to combat those societal structures, policies, and hierarchies that limit access to resources based on group or individual characteristics, including age, race, ethnicity, social class, poverty, religion, gender, immigration status, sexual orientation, and language. (Kenny & Romano, 2009, p. 23)

Prilleltensky (2012) describes two main types of justice: distributive and procedural. Distributive justice refers to the "fair and equitable allocations of burdens and privileges, rights and responsibilities, and pains and gains in society" (p. 6). Procedural justice pertains to "fair, transparent, informative, respectful, and . . . participatory decision making processes" (p. 7). In other words, distributive justice is concerned with *outcomes* (e.g., who has access to resources), and procedural justice is concerned with *process* (e.g., how decisions are made regarding access to resources). Prilleltensky argues that these aspects of justice are directly related to well-being; individuals and communities who experience optimal conditions of justice are more likely to thrive, while those who experience persisting conditions of injustice will suffer.

Prevention initiatives that reflect a social justice perspective aim to reduce social inequality and empower participants. Furthermore, prevention practices should be culturally relevant and adapted for the particular context where they will be implemented.

Consider our example of preventing high school dropout given the following context: A local high school implemented a strict truancy policy. After accruing 5 days of unexcused absences in a semester, students receive a failing grade in all of their classes, even if they are able to satisfactorily make up the work they missed. However, if an engaged parent calls the school to explain the absences, the failing grade will likely be reversed. This policy jeopardizes students' ability to graduate, especially those students with fewer resources. These students may accrue more absences due to factors such as transportation problems or lack of adequate health care. Furthermore, if parents' own experiences in school were unpleasant and were characterized by an unyielding, authoritarian communication style on the part of school officials, they likely will not feel empowered to act on behalf of their children. In this case, prevention efforts informed by a social justice perspective may include lobbying for this policy to be changed and assisting parents in advocating for their children.

System-Centered and Person-Centered Perspectives on Prevention

Prevention initiatives can be focused on enacting system-level change and/ or individual-level change. As discussed earlier, Gordon emphasized change at the system level. For example, system-level prevention strategies aimed at preventing tobacco use may include efforts to limit advertising, to increase taxes on cigarettes, and to outlaw smoking in public places. A person-centered strategy may include a parenting class to help parents know how to talk to their children about tobacco and drug use.

System-centered approaches to prevention often aim to improve the underlying conditions that contribute to illness and dysfunction, such as poverty, injustice, lack of quality education, and limited access to adequate health care. Environmental causes can substantially contribute to the development of mental health problems. For example, we are developing a greater understanding of the connection between the availability of healthy, affordable food and mental health outcomes. When populations chronically lack access to fresh, nutritious food at affordable prices, it is difficult to maintain physical and mental health. System-centered approaches are appropriate in cases where this problem is primarily due to economic and political reasons (i.e., fruits and vegetables are more expensive to grow and transport than junk food).

However, changes aimed at the individual level are also important in the field of prevention. Person-centered prevention interventions involve working directly with people to enhance their competencies and to help them manage life. Counselors, psychologists, and others in the helping professions typically undertake these types of interventions. For example, a preventive intervention related to limited access to healthy food may entail developing recipes using low-cost, nutritious ingredients that are widely available (i.e., dried beans, canned fish) or teaching people how to grow a small vegetable garden in a limited space. The most impactful interventions will be culturally sensitive (e.g., adapting recipes that are familiar to the targeted population) and take into account the specific community context (e.g., suggesting vegetables that can grow given the living situations of intended audience and the region of the country). Other person-centered prevention interventions include counseling groups for people managing stressful situations (e.g., loss of job, divorce) and activities to enhance wellness, resiliency, and problem-solving skills (e.g., conflict resolution training for middle school students).

Two Recent Definitions of Prevention

In this section, we present two newer definitions related to prevention. These definitions are reflective of the three perspectives on prevention we just discussed: prevention and health promotion, prevention and social justice, and prevention at the system level and individual level.

Romano and Hage (2000a)

Romano and Hage (2000a) provide a definition of preventive interventions. They argue that preventive interventions meet one or more of the following criteria.

The intervention

- stops a problem from ever occurring;
- delays the onset of a problem behavior;
- reduces the impact of an existing problem behavior;
- strengthens knowledge, attitudes, and behaviors that promote emotional and physical well-being; and/or
- supports institutional, community, and government policies that promote physical and emotional well-being. (Romano & Hage, 2000a, pp. 740–741)

This definition includes a health promotion focus; interventions "promote emotional and physical well-being." Furthermore, efforts aimed at improving "institutional, community, and government policies" would encompass a social justice framework (although social justice is not explicitly mentioned). Finally, we see that the definition targets both the individual (i.e., "knowledge, attitudes, and behavior") and community levels.

Conyne (2004b)

Conyne (2004b) provided a definition of prevention for use in the fields of counseling and mental health:

Prevention is a goal for both everyday life and service delivery, through which people become empowered to interact effectively and appropriately within varying levels of systems (micro, meso, exo, and macro) and in settings (individual, family, school, community, work). Preventive application can yield a reduction in the occurrence of new cases of a problem, in the duration and severity of incipient problems, and it can promote strengths and optimal human functioning. (Conyne, 2004b, p. 25)

You will notice that this definition is quite broad. First, prevention is defined as a goal, rather than a process or method. Second, the definition includes the concept of everyday prevention; prevention is a goal for "everyday life." Everyday prevention encompasses developing a sense of hope, optimism, and personal strength that buffers against the deleterious consequences of the dings and knocks of life. Conyne's definition emphasizes health promotion and fits with a social justice perspective; prevention empowers people to "interact effectively and appropriately within varying levels of systems . . . and in settings" (p. 25). Furthermore, the definition embraces efforts aimed at the systemwide and the individual levels.

> ### Activity
>
> Define what prevention is, being sure to stress its systemic, ecological, community, and multidisciplinary elements (among others).

4 Competencies Needed for Prevention Proficiency

As the definition of prevention clarifies, it becomes more possible to identify what it takes to implement it. This is a question of competencies—what attitudes, knowledge, skills, and values are necessary for proficient preventive practice? In turn, once competencies are targeted, then training programs, or aspects of existing programs, can be developed to teach those competencies. It follows that if prevention training is lacking or, worse, missing from academic programs, then graduates will be unprepared to deliver prevention interventions once in the field.

The competency domains for preventive practice have been quite clearly charted, however. They "lurk" awaiting broader-scale adoption by academic programs in the helping fields.

What are the practice competencies that are needed by mental health staff to learn and deliver prevention competencies? This section is adapted from the extensive review of prevention training by Conyne et al. (2008). Authors in various fields (prevention science, counseling and counseling psychology, community psychology, violence prevention, clinical training) have contributed to an understanding of this topic, including, but not limited to, Conyne (1987, 1997, 2004a), Romano and Hage (2000a), Ingram (2005), Matthews (2003, 2004), Snyder and Elliott (2005), Cowen (1977), Price (1983), Zolik (1983), Sege and Hoffman (2005), Eddy, Smith, Brown, and Reid (2005), Conyne et al. (2008), and Meers, Werch, Hedrick, and Lepper (1995).

Due to space limitations, we have selected the following sets of prevention competencies from only two of the above sources—(1) prevention science and (2) counseling and counseling psychology. They can be taken as illustrative of the foundation skills thought by experts to be necessary for conducting effective prevention programs. Once presented, we will suggest a supraorganizing framework for organizing prevention competencies.

Prevention Competencies From
a Prevention Science Perspective

Based on an extensive interview and survey process with prevention scientists from several fields, Eddy et al. (2005) identified 13 areas judged to be important for prevention training:

1. *History and context of prevention efforts:* History of prevention programs and research in the United States and throughout the world and knowledge of important people and progress made in prevention

2. *Basic research:* Knowledge of research from the core sciences, theory and research of mental health, resiliency, and health promotion

3. *Program design:* How to develop a preventive intervention and prevention research projects

4. *Developmental timing of interventions:* Building life course timing and life transitions into delivery of developmentally appropriate preventive interventions

5. *Gender and culture issues:* Including competencies of relevant communities to improve the success of preventive interventions

6. *Scientific collaboration on projects:* Including collaborative agenda from within and across departments, institutions, and scientific disciplines

7. *Community collaboration on projects:* Developing and maintaining relationships with study communities and partnering with them to design, deliver, and evaluate projects

8. *Design of preventive intervention trials:* Conceptualizing, planning, and executing methodologically sound controlled prevention trials

9. *Funding of prevention science:* Information about how to acquire sources of funding support for prevention efforts

10. *Administration and management skills:* Using practical management skills for organizing and delivering prevention programs

11. *Economic analysis of preventive impact:* Measuring and analyzing costs and benefits of programs and communicating results clearly

12. *Program evaluation:* Qualitative and quantitative data collections and analyses of prevention interventions

13. *Ethics:* Dealing with ethical dilemmas in all the above areas, and other issues, such as who controls data and program decisions.

Prevention Competencies From a Counseling and Counseling Psychology Perspective

Lewis and Lewis (1977, 1983) initiated consideration of prevention competencies in counseling and counseling psychology. They identified three clusters:

1. *Education:* Instructional strategies to effectively impart information and actively involve participants in order to improve their knowledge and functioning

2. *Program development:* Ability to design and deliver effective prevention programs

3. *Change agentry:* Skills and attitudes needed to foster progressive change in human systems that thwart growth and development.

Matthews and Skowron (2004) adapted this basic set of competency clusters to include the following areas:

(a) *Science and practice of prevention:* Skills in prevention need to be contexualized within a strong science base, where what is done is guided by evidence.

(b) *Ethical and multicultural:* Skills are needed in involving members of the target population, addressing cultural differences in the experience of mental health and mental illness, acknowledging cultural sources of resiliency, and respecting cultural and diversity values when designing programs.

(c) *Program development, programming strategies, and evaluation:* Skills need to be learned in assessing community needs, strategies included within the prevention program itself, and a plan for empirical evaluation of the program.

Britner and O'Neil (2008) and O'Neil and Britner (2008) suggest that teaching prevention—and by extension, doing prevention—includes giving attention to a problem-solving process model and to three frameworks:

1. A "before-the-fact" orientation, differentiating primary prevention from intervention so that skills taught and later used emerge from the appropriate operational context

2. A multidisciplinary focus where inquiry obtains along with a desire to access and use knowledge arising outside one's own discipline (as well as from within it)

3. A social justice perspective that hinges on a social change and humanitarian ethos.

Conyne (1987, 1997, 2004a) evolved a set of prevention competencies over a number of years, drawing from assessments and recommendations of students in his Preventive Counseling course and melding these suggestions with the existing professional literature. A group of 13 competency domains resulted, including the following abilities:

1. *Primary prevention perspective:* To understand and appreciate before-the-fact orientation, reduction of incidence, healthy/at-risk targets, and empowerment

2. *Personal attributes and behaviors:* To be persistent, flexible, and organized

3. *Educational skills:* To set educational goals, select appropriate training materials and formats, involve individuals in active learning, involve groups in active learning, provide clear feedback

4. *Program development skills:* To assess ecological needs, define a problem, identify attainable objectives, develop a variety of intervention options, plan and coordinate detailed implementation, evaluate process and outcomes of program implementation

5. *Change agent skills:* To recognize the need for change in a given system, analyze system resources for change, work effectively as a member of change-oriented teams, advocate for target, negotiate for change

6. *Ethical skills:* To implement ethical code, protect privacy of targets, involve target members

7. *Marketing skills:* To appropriately promote, use telecommunications, appreciate/apply social marketing strategies

8. *Multicultural skills:* To be aware of own cultural values/biases, be aware of target's worldview, apply multicultural awareness and skills appropriately

9. *Group facilitation skills:* To perform core group work skills, lead a team, be a good group member

10. *Collaborative skills:* To function interdependently, problem solve with others, include others' expertise, synthesize diverse inputs

11. *Organization and setting skills:* To gain access to environments, apply organizational development principles and processes

12. *Trend and political dynamic skills:* To understand public policy, respond to system supports and barriers, and predict future trends

13. *Research and evaluation skills:* To assess, design research, apply statistical methods, use data programmatically, write grants, and evaluate social validity.

Romano and Hage (2000c) delineated eight training domains for prevention in psychology:

1. *Community and multidisciplinary collaboration:* To learn roles and needs of community agencies; to understand the philosophical foundations, knowledge bases, and common practices of disciplines and specialties outside counseling psychology; and to develop group leadership skills to facilitate group cohesion, productivity, and teamwork

2. *Knowledge of social and political history:* To learn the history and etiology of social problems, to become knowledgeable about the relationship between contemporary problems and their political and social histories, to learn how groups have been disempowered through racism and social and political discriminatory practices, and to develop an awareness of the social and political realities that place individuals and groups at risk for psychological dysfunction

3. *Protective factors and risk reduction strategies:* To learn the relationship of protective and risk factors for individuals and groups, to develop skills to implement risk reduction strategies, and to develop skills to promote protective factors for individuals and groups

4. *Systemic interventions:* To learn models of system theory and frameworks for interventions, to learn how the social dynamics of institutions and organizations affect individuals, to develop system intervention skills to promote institutional change, and to use group leadership skills, including group process and group dynamic dimensions

5. *Understanding of political and social environments:* To develop an appreciation for political and social contextual factors that affect institutional settings, communities, and neighborhoods; to examine how individuals and groups experience discrimination in specific environments; to learn to identify sources of power and influence in specific environments and intervene to promote psychological well-being; and to learn group leadership skills and advocacy

6. *Psychoeducational groups:* To learn to identify environments and populations that lend themselves to psychoeducational interventions and to learn how to plan, deliver, and assess outcomes of psychoeducational interventions for specific populations and concerns

7. *Prevention research and evaluation:* To learn needs assessment and program evaluation skills; to use quantitative and qualitative research methodologies; to develop longitudinal, epidemiological, and experimental research design skills; to expand the array of disorders and social units studied across the life span; to participate in multidisciplinary and collaborative research that addresses systemic and institutional change; and to learn effective dissemination practices to inform relevant audiences and policy makers

8. *Prevention ethics:* To attend to issues of social equity and justice in prevention practices and science, to adhere to prevention protocol to increase awareness and knowledge about issues of diversity in the practice and science of prevention, and to become familiar with ethical issues and dilemmas in disciplines other than psychology.

A Suggested Supraorganizing Framework for Organizing Prevention Competencies

The foregoing five sets of defined competencies in prevention are in considerable agreement. Together, they form the foundation for a prevention pedagogy in counseling and counseling psychology with broad implications for other related fields. Moreover, building on the work of Albee (1986) and others, Hage et al. (2007) suggest, among many other points, that social justice links substantially with prevention. Social justice entails attention to strengthening or empowering individuals, families, and communities as well as reducing those oppressive social structures and policies that create and sustain social inequities (Albee, 1986; Prilleltensky & Nelson, 1997).

Can these highly interconnected conceptions of prevention competencies be coalesced? We present next a kind of "supra" organizing framework, based on these sets of competencies, in an effort to streamline and make this information more accessible. We hasten to admit that others who may take up this same charge no doubt would produce varying but equally valid (or, alas, even better) syntheses.

Nonetheless, we offer the following framework for consideration. It distills the wide range of prevention competencies presented above into 15, assigning them to 4 traditional domains of curriculum competencies: Knowledge, Skills, Attitudes, and Values.

Prevention Competencies Organized by Domains of Knowledge, Skills, Attitudes, and Values

Knowledge

  History and science of prevention

  Systemic-ecological vantage point

  Multidisciplinary sources of influence

  Incidence reduction, protective and risk factors

  Social justice

Skills

  Basic helping

  Group work, collaboration, consultation

(Continued)

(Continued)

    Organization, community, and ecological development

    Advocacy, change agentry

    Multicultural, diversity

    Ethical, best practice

    Research, program development and evaluation, funding acquisition

    Outreach, marketing

Attitudes

    Personal attributes sensitive to prevention (e.g., persistence, tolerance, long-range view)

Values

    Primary prevention perspective

The "Big Five" in Prevention: Our Nomination _____

You have noticed that we have five general prevention competencies in bold letters: two from the knowledge domain and one from each of the other domains of skills, attitudes, and values. Similar to the "big five" traits in personality assessment (e.g., Goldberg, 1993), although without the empirical support at present, we nominate the following five factors as essential to all prevention efforts. Admittedly, it is difficult to emphasize any one of the competencies, because all of them are involved in conducting effective prevention practice. We suspect that experts would vary on the relative weight accorded to each competency and, in fact, to which competencies should be included in the first place.

Yet our review yields the following "Big Five." We would be very interested in learning your thoughts on this matter.

Primary Prevention Perspective (Value)

This is the most obviously important competency area, and it is a value, a kind of overarching perspective, that serves to guide and to harness energies aimed at preventive ends. A primary prevention perspective is fundamentally important because its contents (before-the-fact vantage point, incidence reduction approach, strengths-oriented emphasis, systemic-ecological foundation) function as a lens through which interactions within human systems can be viewed. That lens, in fact, not only clarifies what is viewed but also redefines and refocuses mental health methods on goals of prevention and promotion.

Most prevention competencies are generic, usable just as well to serve remedial purposes, too. The primary prevention perspective, however, shifts the application of helper competencies from later to earlier, from correction to promotion, from deficits to strengths, and from individual- to community-level applications.

Systemic-Ecological Vantage Point (Knowledge)

Prevention goals are reached through mobilizing resources existing within webs of interconnection. Human settings, relationships, support systems, networks, and person–environment interactions represent key webs of interconnection. Prevention programs strengthen individuals and their interactions with others and with the major environments of their lives—work, school, family, community. The fulcrum for change is found in dynamic systems and the connections (or lack of connections) occurring among members.

Social Justice (Knowledge)

Albee (1986) introduced discussion of the powerful contribution of social pathogens to mental health dysfunction, pointing to the value of prevention strategies targeting the reduction of those pathogens while increasing personal and social system strengths and supports. Examples of social pathogens include poverty, limited access to health care, oppression, racism, sexual harassment, and exploitation. Instances involving the cyber bullying of gay youth, sometimes even contributing to their suicide, provide one appalling example of social injustice in practice. Prevention as social justice (e.g., Kenny et al., 2009) needs to be an important element of any prevention project.

Group Work, Collaboration, Consultation (Skills)

These three methods are the dynamos of change in prevention. They are the engine that drives many successful programs because, by definition, they are calibrated to coalesce and drive the dynamics surrounding interconnections and relationships. While these interventions also can be used responsively with effectiveness, as in therapy situations, in prevention, they are well situated to propel, to reach out, and to proactively connect people and resources. They can be used to facilitate existing networks and can be applied to create such networks when none presently exists.

Group skills are based on interdependence. Drawing from those skills that are aimed at joining interactions among people, both collaboration and consultation add direction and purpose: People are joined together to accomplish task–work goals that they create together. These jointly determined work goals, such as a school task force charged with creating a policy on obesity prevention, serve to motivate cooperative energies and the pooling of resources, intermixed to accomplish together what no one entity could hope to do independently.

Personal Attributes Sensitive to Prevention (Attitude)

Attitudes needed to become an effective counselor and therapist are well documented. Consider the necessary and sufficient conditions identified by Carl Rogers (e.g., empathy, positive regard) as a key beginning point. Prevention attributes build on those conditions and add other essential ones that center on maintaining a long-range perspective and a commitment to tolerance and social justice. Patience, persistence, and a blend of a strong process and equally strong task orientation also are necessary attributes. Prevention is not for the faint of heart. Prevention programs take time to develop, to deliver, and to take effect. You need to be into it not only to win it but for the long haul.

Activity

Review the listing of prevention competencies presented earlier. Assess each one in terms of your own level of mastery using a rating scale from 1 to 3, where

1 = *no mastery*, 2 = *some mastery*, and 3 = *mastery*

Identify what you might do to increase mastery in any competencies you have rated a "1" or a "2."

Finally, discuss this information with a colleague.

5 Prevention in Practice

In this section, we provide a detailed example of prevention in the field of youth bullying prevention. Our goal is to elaborate on the concepts that have already been mentioned and introduce additional key characteristics while providing a practical example of how prevention works in practice. Specifically, we highlight the ecological, developmental, and multidisciplinary elements of prevention practice.

Youth Bullying Prevention

Childhood and adolescence should be experienced as a safe and supportive time during which individuals develop and master skills to function productively as adults. The important work of childhood is learning: learning academic content, learning to make and keep friends, learning self-control, learning how to harness one's strengths to work toward a satisfying future, among other goals. However, for many children and adolescents, the experience of growing up is unnecessarily painful. Being the victim of, or witness to, bullying and aggression leads to learning of a different sort: learning to be fearful and self-conscious, learning not to trust adults to be aware of or solve all problems.

Bullying in the United States is widespread, with between 35% and 50% of students reporting experiencing bullying in the current school term (Nansel et al., 2001) or year (Robers, Zhang, & Truman, 2010). The types of mistreatment reported by students in schools include physical aggression (e.g., being hit), verbal abuse (e.g., being belittled), and relational aggression (e.g., being the subject of rumors).

The negative impact of bullying and mistreatment on academic and mental, behavioral, and emotional outcomes is well documented. In a review of the mental health literature, Arseneault, Bowes, and Shakoor (2010) reported that the following outcomes are associated with being the victim of bullying: increased social isolation, depression, anxiety, self-harm behaviors (including suicide thoughts and attempts), aggressive behaviors (including weapon carrying), and psychotic symptoms. Furthermore, they report that the consequences of being bullied can be long term and continue into adulthood, including increased rates of psychiatric symptoms and criminal offenses.

In addition to adverse consequences for individual students, mistreatment is also costly in terms of schoolwide impact. Phillips, Linney, and Pack (2008) identified costs of mistreatment at the school level, including loss of instructional time, reduced staff morale and increased turnover, and increased financial costs associated with heightened security. Given the widespread impact and serious outcomes associated with youth bullying and aggression, prevention efforts are critical. Fortunately, bullying research has been the subject of substantial interest in recent years, and funding opportunities have been made available for prevention efforts. Therefore, our understanding of this relatively complex phenomenon has been improving, although there is still much to be learned. In the next section, we describe what we know about how bullying behaviors develop. We will use an ecological framework to describe multiple levels of influences, and we will highlight the interplay between risk and protective factors on the development of bullying behaviors.

The Ecological Model and Risk and Protective Factors

In 1979, Bronfenbrenner authored an influential text, *The Ecology of Human Development*, which provides a useful framework for considering prevention. The beauty of his model is its comprehensiveness. The ecological model has the ability to incorporate different explanations of how problems develop into a single theoretical perspective. Bronfenbrenner argued that human behavior is a function of the interaction between the person and the environment, and he particularly emphasized the importance of context. The same individual in two different environments may behave in markedly different ways. The ecological model provides a framework for considering the variety of contexts in which we are immersed.

The ecological model can be conceptualized as a set of concentric ellipses beginning with individual characteristics and working outward to family, community, and cultural levels. Figure 5.1 provides an example of how the ecological model can be used to describe the factors that influence the development of bullying behaviors across multiple levels of influence. Within and across each level, individual and contextual factors interact to influence behavior. Risk factors increase the likelihood that an individual will engage in an undesirable behavior (in our case, bullying). Protective factors, on the other hand, reduce the likelihood that a person will engage in harmful behavior. Historically, risk factors have received the bulk of research attention; however, as more researchers acknowledge the importance of positive influences on warding off problems, the examination of protective factors has increased.

Our goals are to (a) provide a sample of the types of risk and protective factors at multiple levels that influence the propensity to engage in problem

Figure 5.1 Protective and Risk Factors Associated With Bullying Behaviors

Protective Factors

Socially competent

Has a sense of purpose in life

Displays positive values: honesty, friendship, peace, & respect

Connected to school & friends

Values learning

Loving and caring

Positive communication

Clear rules and consequences

Appropriate supervision

Model respect and peaceful conflict resolution

Involved and interested in child's life

Positive school climate

Good relationships between teachers and students

Clear policies against bullying

High expectations for all students

Appropriate supervision

Excellence in teaching

Opportunities for meaningful participation

Students don't accept aggression in others

Opportunities for youths to meaningfully participate in community activities (sports, educational programs, volunteer opportunities)

Safe, supervised areas available for all children

Attitudes toward children are caring and supportive

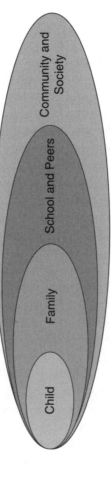

Child

Family

School and Peers

Community and Society

Risk Factors

Holds beliefs that support aggression

Has successfully used aggression in the past

Does not expect negative consequences when using aggression

Lacks problem solving skills

Exhibits other high risk behavior (e.g., drug use)

Attributes aggression to others where there is none

Negative relationship with the child, including rejection

Poor communication

No consequences for negative behaviors

Lack of supervision

Parents support the use of aggression

Problems in the family are solved with aggression

Negative school climate

Adults think bullying is "no big deal"

Lacks or does not enforce rules against bullying

Few opportunities for students who need help academically or socially

Students value aggression, think aggression is cool or funny

Culture supports violence

High levels of violence portrayed in the media

Lack of safe, supervised areas

Access to firearms is easy

Children/youths often viewed with suspicion

behaviors and (b) suggest ways in which prevention programs may enhance protective factors and reduce risk factors. We use childhood bullying and aggression as an example but hope you will consider how the ecological model may be used with the prevention applications that are of interest to you.

The information presented in this example is adapted from *Bullying Prevention: Creating a Positive School Climate and Developing Social Competence* (Orpinas & Horne, 2006), and it is not intended to be exhaustive. For a more thorough examination of the risk and protective factors pertaining to bullying, see Orpinas and Horne (2006).

The Individual Level

Characteristics at the individual level contribute to the likelihood that a young person will engage in bullying behaviors. These characteristics include attitudes, beliefs, skills, and experiences. For instance, students are more likely to engage in aggression if they have successfully used violence to get what they want in the past, and they believe that they will face no negative consequences of aggressive behaviors. On the other hand, students who hold positive values such as honesty, friendship, peace, and respect will be less likely to act in aggressive ways.

Some risk and protective factors can be thought of as two sides of the same coin. For example, a student who is socially competent and has a vast store of peaceful conflict resolution techniques can be thought of as representing one side of a continuum. At the other side of the continuum is the student who lacks social and problem-solving skills and uses violence out of frustration. Other risk and protective factors don't have a natural corollary. For example, a student who exhibits a special talent (e.g., being a gifted musician) may derive a sense of identity and purpose that protects against engaging in violence. However, lacking such extraordinary skill should not be considered a risk factor for aggression.

It is worth noting that some risk and protective factors are malleable and some are fixed. For example, being male is associated with increased risk of engaging in bullying, but this is not a modifiable risk factor. Effective preventive interventions should target risk and protective factors that are changeable. The example of gender also underscores the point that risk factors do not *cause* a person to become aggressive. Not all boys are bullies. However, risk factors do increase the likelihood that an individual will engage in aggressive behaviors.

Preventive Interventions at the Individual Level

Many preventive interventions for bullying have targeted individual characteristics. These interventions aim to bolster protective factors while reducing risk factors. For example, the Bully Busters series (elementary school: Horne, Bartolomucci, & Newman-Carlson, 2003; middle school: Newman, Horne, & Bartolomucci, 2000; family: Horne, Lind Whitford, & Bell, 2008) includes activities to help students learn positive ways to deal with anger, diffuse conflict, and act in assertive, rather than in aggressive, ways. The program also addresses beliefs about bullying, helping students understand that engaging in bullying rarely leads to satisfactory outcomes (even if the aggressive student does experience a short-term benefit). Other effective ways to assist students who bully include developing social, communication, and problem-solving skills.

The Family Level

Family life, including the characteristics of parents and siblings, the relationship among family members, and family routines and rules, all impact the propensity to develop bullying behaviors. Major risk factors at the family level include parental aggression, parental rejection, and lack of parental monitoring. Positive parenting, on the other hand, is hugely protective against all manner of childhood problem behaviors, including aggression. Positive parenting is characterized as a parent–child relationship that is warm and accepting, with open communication, where the parent exhibits interest in and has high expectations for the child. A major component of positive parenting is being present and engaged and sharing in the highs and lows of everyday life.

Preventive Interventions at the Family Level

Because parents are so influential on the lives of their children, parenting groups have been an important strategy for preventing and reducing bullying behaviors. The GREAT Schools and Families Program (The Multisite Violence Prevention Project, 2008) asked teachers to identify sixth-grade students who were at high risk for engaging in bullying. These students and their parents were asked to participate in family groups to gain skills and strategies to prevent future aggressive behavior. Participants discussed strategies for solving conflicts, managing anger and other emotions, and setting appropriate limits and boundaries for their children, among other topics.

At this point in our example, we can begin to see how risk and protective factors interact with each other both within and across levels of the ecological model. Individual characteristics of the child may interact with characteristics of the parents to affect parenting style. For example, some children are more likely to test the limits of what they can get away with, and parents will respond in different ways—some may become overly strict, some may simply give up, and others may develop more effective ways to parent. In developing preventive interventions, these types of interactions should be considered.

The School/Peer Level

How schools are organized and run has a major impact on the amount of bullying that takes place. Orpinas and Horne (2006) describe the eight components of positive school climate. Together, these components describe a school that will be resistant to the development of bullying behaviors. The components are excellence in teaching, positive school values, awareness of strengths and problems, appropriate policies and accountability, caring and respect, positive expectations, teacher support, and a physical environment that promotes learning. The components are presented in Figure 5.2.

The attitudes, beliefs, and actions of peers are also influential on the likelihood of an individual engaging in aggressive behaviors. Here, we group the peer and the school level together, because the school climate is a critical component in what students think is acceptable. For example, a student will be more likely to engage in aggression if classmates regularly cheer on fights and assign high status to bullies. However, it is possible for schools to establish policies and values to counteract these attitudes and behaviors. Given a positive school climate, the influence of peers will promote healthy interactions among students rather than aggression.

Figure 5.2　Eight Components of Positive School Climate

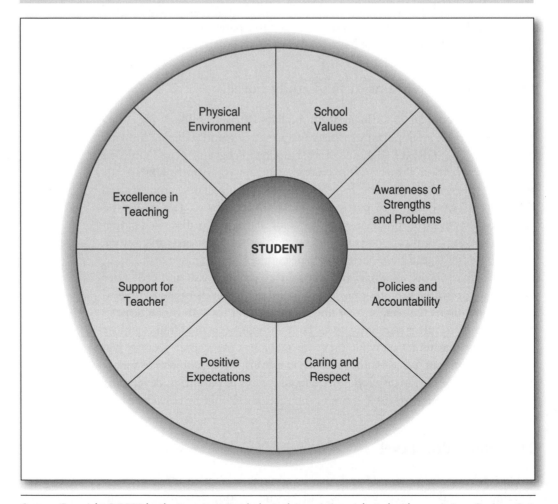

Source: Copyright © 2005 by the American Psychological Association. Adapted with permission. Orpinas, P. & Horne, A. (2005). *Bullying Prevention: Creating a Positive School Climate and Developing Social Competence.* The use of APA information does not imply endorsement by APA.

Preventive Interventions at the School Level

Many antibullying efforts have been geared toward the school level. After all, students spend a large portion of the day in school, and it is an efficient way to reach a large number of young people. School-level interventions have targeted students, teachers, and the school environment as a whole. The Bully Busters series (Horne et al., 2003; Newman, et al., 2000) is primarily geared at teachers, with a recommended option of whole-school implementation. Effective preventive interventions work to enhance the components of positive school climate.

It is worth mentioning here that people involved in prevention activities benefit from considering what they are trying to do and what they actually have influence over. When we work with teachers in schools, we ask them to list the factors that contribute to the use of aggression by their students. The list may look something like this:

- Lives in bad neighborhood
- Hallways during class changes are too crowded
- Violent video games
- Lack of parental supervision
- Lacks skills to get along with other students

Given this list, the teacher really only has influence on two of these factors: the crowded hallways and the student's lack of social skills. When we work with teachers on this activity we help them identify their "sphere of influence"—that is, what can they change, what is beyond their impact? Class changing procedures can be modified, and teachers can help students learn better social skills; what teachers can't do very effectively is move all students to better neighborhoods, change the content of video games, or force parents to supervise their children more. These factors belong to other levels of the ecological model (e.g., bad neighborhoods are a risk factor at the community level) and are generally outside the teacher's sphere of influence.

The Community/Society Level

Community and societal factors are related to the amount of bullying that young people experience. When young people live in safe communities that provide enriching activities (e.g., sports, educational, and volunteer programs), they are less likely to engage in aggression, delinquency, and other problem behaviors. On the other hand, when young people live in unsafe environments and have few constructive options to occupy their free time, aggressive behaviors are more likely to develop.

Cross-national studies have demonstrated that rates of bullying vary widely internationally. Societal factors, such as cultural values toward violence and the availability of firearms and other weapons, influence these rates. Furthermore, the economic and social structure of a society may contribute to youth aggression. The economic, political, and social structures that contribute to a fair and just society are the same forces that protect against the development of aggression in children.

Preventive Interventions at the Community/Society Level

To this point, our examples of preventive interventions have mainly been person centered rather than system centered. Here we shift focus. Prevention at the community and society level are necessarily system centered. We previously talked about how teachers don't have much influence over the quality of the neighborhood where students live. Prevention activities need to be focused at the community and society level to take on this type of risk factor. At the community level, efforts to prevent bullying may include efforts to reduce crime within the community, increase economic opportunities, and expand after-school and other community programs (e.g., Boys and Girls clubs, nature camp, sports leagues). Avenues for young people to contribute meaningfully to their own community are also impactful, such as volunteer opportunities, youth art exhibitions, and the like.

At the society level, prevention activities may entail efforts to enhance social justice. A fair and just society provides the foundation for children to develop in healthy, positive ways. Efforts that alleviate poverty and otherwise address structural inequality should help foster more nurturing environments for children's development.

On a more limited scale, media campaigns may help change attitudes and beliefs about aggression and violence. For example, MTV recently launched the website A Thin Line (n.d.; http://www.athinline.org/) to encourage healthy attitudes about the uses of communication technology. The website focuses on combating cyberbullying and digital dating abuse. These types of campaigns may help counteract the negative messages so often encountered through the media by young people (e.g., violent song lyrics, movies, etc.).

Preventive Interventions Across Levels of the Ecological Model

The most effective preventive interventions are likely those which target risk and protective factors across levels of the ecological model. An anti-bullying campaign that includes individual, family, school, and community level elements will likely be more impactful than one that only targets one of these levels. This type of campaign may start at the school level. School administrators may determine that bullying is a problem and develop a plan to improve the school climate. Part of this plan may include having teachers present antibullying lessons in class. Students who are at higher risk for being the perpetrator or victim of bullying may need to receive individual attention from a school counselor or psychologist. After-school parenting classes can help enhance protective factors and reduce risk factors at the family level. Finally, administrators may reach out to the community for additional support, for example, to improve options for supervised, meaningful after-school activities. This type of comprehensive program is likely to be more powerful than an intervention that is more limited or scattershot.

Developmental Perspectives on Preventive Interventions

Although the ecological model is comprehensive, a potential weakness is that it does not explicitly address developmental changes through time. Prevention efforts should take into account the developmental stage of the intended participants, both in terms of age and in terms of the readiness of participants to engage in change.

In Chapter 1 of this book, we discussed how mental, behavioral, emotional, and substance use problems often develop at a young age. Prevention efforts must begin early as well. In the case of bullying, aggressive behaviors tend to increase throughout elementary school and peak during middle school. The social skills needed to get along with others peacefully can be learned from a young age. However, bullying may occur across the life span, and antibullying campaigns should be targeted for the developmental level of the intended participants. Prevention in elementary school will look different from prevention in high school, and prevention in adult settings (e.g., workplace bullying) will carry a different set of considerations. Furthermore, efforts to improve maternal heath and infant care represent a promising path to improve a variety of educational and mental health outcomes, including the reduction of bullying.

Another important developmental consideration is the readiness of the participant to engage in change. The Stages of Change model (Prochaska & Di Clemente, 1982) offers a theoretical perspective on how people go about changing behavior. It provides important insights for prevention because prevention often involves asking people to change behavior, whether it be exercising more, wearing a helmet, or using a new strategy for relaxation. The steps leading to sustained change are as follows:

- *Precontemplation:* not aware that change may be needed
- *Contemplation:* considering change, but not ready to act
- *Preparation:* decided that change is needed
- *Action:* taking action to change
- *Maintenance:* taking action to sustain change long term

Preventive interventions should consider these stages as they relate to the intended audience. For example, when working to prevent bullying in schools, some teachers are already committed and taking steps to respond to bullying; others are clueless that the problem exists or think that teachers can't make a difference to stop bullying. The techniques used to reach these groups of teachers will need to be tailored to their unique needs.

The Ecological Model and a Developmental Perspective: Implications for Prevention

Several implications for prevention emerge from our tour of the ecological model and our consideration of a developmental perspective on prevention.

- To be effective, preventive interventions may need to target multiple areas of the ecological model. The development of problem behaviors is often complicated with roots in different levels of the ecological model. Risk and protective factors interact both within and across levels of influence.
- Preventive programs are more likely to succeed when a developmental perspective is employed. Developmental factors related to age and readiness to change should be considered.
- Effective prevention efforts benefit from a multidisciplinary team for the reasons stated above. It is unlikely that one researcher will have all of the necessary knowledge and skills to develop and implement an impactful prevention program. Therefore, we recommend that those interested in prevention reach out to others, particularly in different but complementary fields, to increase the likelihood for success.

Activity

Capture in your mind an event that involves a lot of moving parts: for example, a large wedding, a Thanksgiving dinner for 20 at your house, organizing a national conference, delivering a substance abuse prevention program. Or something else that comes to you . . .

What allows your chosen event to be successful? How does it happen? Who does what? What roles and responsibilities are involved? How do people interrelate? How are resources acquired? How are time lines involved?

Write a one-page detailed scenario, using the questions just above to guide you.

Do you notice how collaboration runs through the activities? How?

6 Some Possible Directions

At the macrolevel, national health care reform has been signed into law by the President in the form of the Patient Protection and Affordable Care Act (2010). A National Prevention Strategy called for by this Act was issued June 16, 2011, and it will be summarized below. A second Act, the Health Care and Education Reconciliation Act of 2010, gave specific attention to health care and education intersections. These instances of legislative activity occurring at the national level in the United States indicate that prevention is assuming an increasingly important level of significance in health care. The following discussion underscores the inevitable connection of prevention with political processes.

On June 16, 2011, a National Prevention Strategy was released by the federal government. Called for by the Affordable Care Act, Kathleen Sebelius, the Secretary of the Department of Health and Human Services, indicated that the strategy "will help us transform our health care system away from a focus on sickness and disease to a focus on prevention and wellness."

The National Prevention Strategy is based on collaboration between public and private partners. It is aimed at helping American citizens remain healthy and fit as a way to improve the nation's prosperity. Four strategic directions are contained in the national approach; you may note that these strategies contain elements, which we have considered earlier, that are important for prevention, including collaboration, community focus, social ecology, early care, empowerment, and social justice.

1. *Building healthy and safe community environments:* Prevention of disease is not contained to the doctor's office, but it starts in our communities and at home.

2. *Expanding quality preventive services in both clinical and community settings:* Improved health, accompanied by lower health care costs, is achieved with people receiving preventive care such as immunizations and cancer screenings.

3. *Empowering people to make healthy choices:* People can become empowered to make better and healthier life choices when they have access to easy-to-understand and actionable information and resources.

4. *Eliminating health disparities:* The quality of life for American citizens can be improved by removing disparities standing in the way of achieving and maintaining health.

(For more information about the National Prevention Strategy see: www .HealthCare.gov/news/factsheets/prevention06162011a.html and www.Health Care.gov/center/councils/nphpphc.)

The American Psychological Association's CEO (chief executive officer), Norman Anderson, noted several gains for psychology in health care reform (2010, April 7) in the following broad categories: (a) integrated health care, (b) mental and behavioral health care, (c) *prevention and wellness*, (d) psychology workforce development, (e) *elimination of health disparities*, (f) support for psychological research, and (g) involvement with consumers, families, and caregivers.

Prevention and wellness indicators include eliminating cost sharing for eligible health services; expanding prevention and wellness initiatives targeting depression, elder abuse, and postpartum conditions; and directing the Clinical Preventive Services Task Force to consider best practices presented by scientific societies when developing recommendations. In terms of eliminating health disparities, indicators include collecting data and developing quality measures to proceed in eliminating health disparities and developing a national strategy to improve delivery of health care services and outcomes in patient health.

In a larger sense, the two health care reform Acts are preventive in scope by their very nature, for they are aimed at extending health care coverage to millions of uninsured persons, reducing health care costs for those who do and do not have insurance, and ending discriminatory practices such as pre-existing conditions. The parity provision to equate mental and behavioral health care with medical and surgical services also clearly supports a preventive agenda. These prevention initiatives within the health care reform package build on decades of hard work by countless numbers of researchers, practitioners, advocates, politicians, and citizens.

The most recent report of the U.S. Surgeon General, focusing on the prevention of obesity, clearly documents the essential role of broad-scale prevention practices in promoting optimal health. It further provides a stellar instance of how prevention has taken hold at the highest levels of health policy and research as a key goal and set of strategies in health care. A focus has emerged on interactions of personal behaviors and biological traits with aspects of the physical and social environment and by attention to interventions that can occur in multiple settings.

The relationship among personal behaviors, biological traits, and social and physical environments is being deepened and expanded through exciting studies in the area of neuroscience and epigenetics. Promising and significant advancements will continue to occur in neuroscience as they relate to health research, practice, and training—including prevention. Research conducted with healthy people and with those suffering from certain diseases, such as asthma, demonstrates that exposure to certain environmental stimuli early in life programs biological systems that affect physical health throughout the course of life. One assumes that analogous patterns also may apply to mental and emotional functioning. Thus, this and similar neuroscience research suggest that exposure in early childhood to low socioeconomic status, when patterns of immune responsivity are being developed and established, can become fixed through epigenetic modifications (Chen, 2010). Implications for prevention theory, research, practice, and training remain to be unearthed.

Exciting work in interpersonal neurobiology (Gantt & Cox, 2010) also holds considerable promise for prevention programs, especially those that are based on interpersonal and group delivery formats. Research accumulates to indicate that "human beings are hard-wired to connect with one another throughout life" (Badenoch & Cox, 2010, p. 463). As the work of Siegel (1999, 2010) suggests by extension, prevention programs that serve to stimulate neuronal activation and growth—what he has abbreviated as "SNAG," can promote increased integration of brain activity and contribute to healthier functioning and, one would expect, the prevention of psychopathology.

Advancements in electronic technologies present additional ways through which prevention and promotion activity can be pursued for positive ends. Note, however, as with any technology, adverse uses also can occur. Cyber bullying (we will discuss bullying more extensively in a practice example in the next section) provides a specific example as does the role of various electronic technologies in contributing to a general decline in social civility that many perceive occurring (think of the venom contained in many TV election advertisements as just one example).

Back to the potentially positive influence of electronic technologies, social networking vehicles, such as Facebook and Twitter, among others, allow users to connect and communicate, thus, offering the potential to maintain and enhance relationships virtually. Personal health records, such as those by Google Health, WebMD Health Manager, and Microsoft Healthvault, allow users to monitor and measure a number of health indices, such as cholesterol (Borzo, 2010). Wii applications provide users with opportunities to play sports, such as bowling, downhill skiing, or baseball; and to engage in health promotion exercises, such as yoga and balancing. Senior citizen centers are just one of many settings where Wii is being used to support the health of its users. Smartphone applications are available for mental health professionals to monitor and support clients between sessions and to provide users with the ability to chart their mood, energy level, diet, sleep patterns, and stress management activities (Versel, 2010).

Further developments in health-oriented electronic vehicles and applications can only be expected to occur in the future. Individually based possibilities for prevention, such as are available now, no doubt will expand, and group- and community-based prevention projects in which electronic vehicles are embedded await development; the project by Farson (1972) decades back comes to mind, where an ongoing televised encounter group formed the basis for guided small group discussions that occurred throughout the San Diego community.

How will counseling psychology and other mental health–oriented professions and disciplines mesh with this significant change in the national health care fabric? Momentum is building both within the profession and in health care to support prevention. Counseling psychology has stood rather flat-footed before in its capacity to assertively pursue a prevention agenda. Predictions about "the time for prevention having finally arrived" have fallen far short over the decades (Blocher, 2000; Vera, 2000).

In fact, as noted in the section of this book on "History," prevention in mental health is replete with false starts and with assertions of support unmatched by continuous action. As a result, training and practice in prevention still lag, even though research and scholarly production have been markedly increasing. Among many challenges, we suggest that the major one is that prevention theory, research, training, practice, and advocacy need to be integrated comprehensively and applied consistently. Only then will prevention assume its rightful place in mental health as an effective and potent force for personal and societal change.

7 Coming Attractions

Stay Tuned for Next Books in the Kit

Our goal in this first book in the *Prevention Practice Kit* is to lay a foundation for understanding what we consider to be essential elements of prevention that, if applied well, can lead to highly effective preventive practice. Topics included in the next seven books of this series were carefully selected for their potential to elaborate on these essential elements. In turn, the authors are among the shining stars of the prevention field. The resulting combination of topics and authors yields a blueprint for prevention practice that can guide effective prevention practice—something that is keenly needed.

A thumbnail sketch of each book follows:

Book 2: *Best Practices in Prevention*, by Sally Hage, PhD, and John Romano, PhD

Practical steps need to be considered by prevention practitioners as they engage with others in developing and delivering prevention projects. In this book, the authors draw from the latest work in prevention best practices to highlight the essential aspects of collaboration, user participation, attention to cultural imperatives, and program dissemination, while attending to often knotty issues surrounding privacy in prevention and promotion efforts.

Book 3: *Social Justice and Culturally Relevant Prevention*, by Elizabeth M. Vera, PhD, and Maureen E. Kenny, PhD

Prevention must be geared to and harness the unique cultural forces present within the population and setting that will constitute the prevention offering. In addition, an important aspect of prevention involves opening opportunities for people to become involved, to gain access to resources, and to influence the course of life events—without infringing on the rights of others. In this book, advocacy and social justice strategies are detailed for preventionists, the implementation of which can lead to empowerment of persons and the improvement of settings. Populations deserving of special attention are given appropriate attention, such as immigrants.

Book 4: *Prevention Groups*, by Elaine Clanton Harpine, PhD

This book indicates when prevention groups may be needed and when they are beneficial. It details how to create and deliver prevention groups, one of the most useful forms of person-centered prevention. It emphasizes the necessity to incorporate group processes within these groups, in addition to salient content, and it will clarify prevention group distinctions between in therapy and prevention. It gives particular attention to groups in school settings that are used to reach prevention goals.

Book 5: *Prevention and Consultation*, by A. Michael Dougherty, PhD

Consultation is a strategically valuable indirect prevention intervention by itself and is an integral part of nearly every other direct program. This book describes how preventionists can conceptualize and deliver consultation to providers and to community members as part of general program development in prevention and as a stand-alone intervention, emphasizing a triadic skills model and the importance of collaborative processes.

Book 6: *Evidence-Based Prevention*, by Katherine A. Raczynski, MA, Michael Waldo, PhD, Jonathan Schwartz, PhD, Arthur M. Horne, PhD

This book provides an introduction to evidence-based prevention in psychology. A broad overview of considerations for evaluating the quality and trustworthiness of prevention research is provided along with a discussion of common features of effective prevention programs. The book provides guidance on identifying evidence-based programs, including detailed descriptions of online registries of prevention programs. The book also provides recommendations for determining the need for a prevention program, selecting and implementing an appropriate program, and evaluating outcomes.

Book 7: *Program Development and Evaluation in Prevention,* by Robert K. Conyne, PhD

This book describes pragmatic and concrete planning and evaluation steps that can lead to sound prevention programs. Attention is given to how programs need to be developed with evaluation in mind and to the necessity for prevention programs to be centered on positive growth and avoidance of negative consequences. It builds on previous work of the author in this area (Conyne, 2010).

Book 8: *Public Policy and Mental Health,* by Emily M. Good and Maureen A. Pirog, PhD

Prevention can often be accomplished most broadly and efficiently through public policy programs. It is an area frequently overlooked by psychologists, counselors, and social workers because public policy is not within the training and skill set of practitioners or professors. This chapter elaborates the relationship between prevention and public policy, giving attention to such matters as cost–benefit analysis, among others.

References _____

Albee, G. (1982). Preventing psychopathology and promoting human potential. *American Psychologist, 37,* 1043–1050.

Albee, G. (1985). The argument for primary prevention. *Journal of Primary Prevention, 5,* 213–219.

Albee, G. (1986). Toward a just society: Lessons from observations on the primary prevention of psychopathology. *American Psychologist, 41,* 891–898.

American Psychological Association. (1999). Archival description of counseling psychology. *The Counseling Psychologist, 27,* 589–592.

Anderson, N. (2010, April 7). *American Psychological Association health care reform activities update.* Retrieved from http://www.apa.org/health-reform/pdf/ceo-update-april-2010.pdf

Arseneault, L., Bowes, L., & Shakoor, S. (2010). Bullying victimization in youths and mental health problems: Much ado about nothing? *Psychological Medicine, 40,* 717–729.

Badenoch, B., & Cox, P. (2010). Integrating interpersonal neurobiology with group psychotherapy. *International Journal of Group Psychotherapy, 60,* 462–482.

Baker, S. B., & Shaw, M. C. (1987). *Improving counseling through primary prevention.* Columbus, OH: Merrill.

Banning, J., & Kaiser, L. (1974). An ecological perspective and model for campus design. *Personnel and Guidance Journal, 52,* 370–375.

Beers, C. W. (1908). *A mind that found itself: An autobiography.* New York, NY: Longmans, Green.

Blocher, D. (1974). Toward an ecology of student development. *Personnel and Guidance Journal, 52,* 360-365.

Blocher, D. (2000). *The evolution of counseling psychology.* New York, NY: Springer.

Borzo, J. (2010, October 25). Tracking your health. *Wall Street Journal,* R-7.

Britner, P., & O'Neil, J. (2008). The teaching of primary prevention: Concluding thoughts and a call to action. *Journal of Primary Prevention, 29,* 455–459.

Bronfenbrenner, U. (1979). *The ecology of human development.* Cambridge, MA: Harvard University Press.

Brown, S., & Lent, R. (Eds.). (2008). *Handbook of counseling psychology* (4th ed.). New York, NY: Wiley.

Bylaws. (2006). *Prevention: A Section of the Division of Counseling Psychology (17) of the American Psychological Association.* Retrieved http://www.div17.org/preventionsection/bylaws.htm

Caplan, G. (1964). *Principles of preventive psychiatry*. New York, NY: Basic Books.

Caplan, G. (1970). *The theory and practice of mental health consultation*. New York, NY: Basic Books.

Chen, E. (2010). Psychological determinants of health laboratory. Retrieved from http://www2.psych.ubc.ca/~healthpsych/edith.htm

Coie, J., Watt, N., West, S., Hawkins, J., Asarnow, J., Markman, H., . . . Long, B. (1993). The science of prevention: A conceptual framework and some directions for a national research program. *American Psychologist, 48,* 1013–1022.

Conyne, R. (1975). Mapping for counselor action. *Personnel & Guidance Journal, 54,* 150–155.

Conyne, R. (1978). An analysis of student-environment mismatches. *Journal of College Student Personnel, 19,* 461–465.

Conyne, R. (1987). *Primary preventive counseling: Empowering people and systems.* Muncie, IN: Accelerated Development.

Conyne, R. (1997). Educating students in preventive counseling. *Counselor Education and Supervision, 36,* 259–269.

Conyne, R. (2000). Prevention in counseling psychology: At long last, has the time now come? *The Counseling Psychologist, 28,* 838–844.

Conyne, R. (2004a). Prevention groups: In J. DeLucia-Waack, D. Gerrity, C. Kalodner, & M. Riva (Eds.), *Handbook of group counseling and psychotherapy* (pp. 621–629). Thousand Oaks, CA: Sage.

Conyne, R. (2004b). *Preventive counseling: Helping people to become empowered in systems and settings* (2nd ed.). New York, NY: Brunner-Routledge.

Conyne, R. (2010). *Prevention program development and evaluation: An incidence reduction, culturally-relevant approach.* Thousand Oaks, CA: Sage.

Conyne, R. (2012). A history of prevention in counseling psychology. In E. Vera (Ed.), *Oxford handbook of prevention* (pp. 16–33). New York, NY: Oxford University Press.

Conyne, R., & Clanton Harpine, E. (Eds.). (2010). Prevention groups: Evidence-based approaches to advance the field [Special issue]. *Group Dynamics: Theory, Research, and Practice, 14,* 193–280.

Conyne, R., & Hage, S. (2009). Prevention groups: In B. Erford (Ed.), *The ACA encyclopedia of counseling* (pp. 406–407). Alexandria, VA: American Counseling Association.

Conyne, R., & Horne, A. (Eds.). (2001). The use of groups for prevention [Special issue]. *Journal for Specialists in Group Work, 26,* 205–292.

Conyne, R., Newmeyer, M., Kenny, M., Romano, J., & Matthews, C. (2008). Two key strategies for teaching prevention: Specialized course and infusion. *Journal of Primary Prevention, 29,* 375–401.

Cowen, E. (1973). Social and community interventions. *Annual Review of Psychology, 24,* 423–472.

Cowen, E. (1977). Baby steps toward primary prevention. *American Journal of Community Psychology, 5,* 1–22.

Cowen, E. (1980). The wooing of primary prevention. *American Journal of Community Psychology, 8,* 254–284.

Cowen, E. (1983). Primary prevention in mental health: Past, present, and future. In R. Felner, L. Jason, J. Moritsugu, & S. Faber (Eds.), *Preventive psychology: Theory, research, and practice* (pp. 11–25). New York, NY: Pergamon.

Cowen, E. (1985). Person-centered approaches to primary prevention in mental health: Situation-focused and competence-enhancement. *American Journal of Community Psychology, 13,* 31–49.

Cowen, E. (2000). Community psychology and routes to psychological wellness. In J. Rappaport & E. Seidman (Eds.), *Handbook of community psychology* (pp. 79–99). New York, NY: Kluwer.

Daher, D., Corazzini, J., & McKinnon, R. (1977). An environmental redesign program for residence halls. *Journal of College Student Personnel, 18,* 11–15.

Drum, D., & Figler, H. (1973). *Outreach in counseling: Applying the growth and prevention model in schools and colleges.* New York, NY: Intext.

Durlak, J. (2003). Effective prevention and health promotion programming. In T. Gullotta & M. Bloom (Eds.), *Encyclopedia of primary prevention and health promotion* (pp. 61–69). New York, NY: Kluwer.

Durlak, J., & Wells, A. (1997). Primary prevention programs for children and adolescents: A meta-analytic review. *American Journal of Community Psychology, 25,* 115–152.

Eddy, J. M., Smith, P., Brown, C. H., & Reid, J. B. (2005). A survey of prevention science training: Implications for educating the next generation. *Prevention Science, 6,* 59–71.

Eisenberg, D., & Neighbors, K. (2007). *Economics of preventing mental disorders and substance abuse among young people.* Paper commissioned by the Committee on Prevention of Mental Disorders and Substance Abuse Among Children, Youth, and Young Adults: Research Advances and Promising Interventions, Board on Children, Youth, and Families, National Research Council and the Institute of Medicine, Washington, DC.

Farson, R. (1972). Self-directed groups and community mental health. In L. Solomon & B. Berzon (Eds.), *New perspectives on encounter groups* (pp. 224–232). San Francisco, CA: Jossey-Bass.

Fouad, N., Gerstein, L., & Toporek, R. (2006). Social justice and counseling psychology in context. In R. Toporek, L. Gerstein, N. Fouad, G. Roysircar, & T. Israel (Eds.), *Handbook for social justice in counseling psychology: Leadership, vision, and action* (pp. 1–17). Thousand Oaks, CA: Sage.

Fretz, B., & Simon, N. (1992). Professional issues in counseling psychology: Continuity, change and challenge. In S. D. Brown & R. W. Lent (Eds.), *Handbook of counseling psychology* (pp. 3–36). New York, NY: Wiley.

Gantt, S., & Cox, P. (Eds.). (2010). Neurobiology and building interpersonal systems: Groups, couples and beyond [Special issue]. *Interpersonal Journal of Group Psychotherapy, 60,* 455–604.

Goldberg, L. (1993). The structure of phenotypic personality traits. *American Psychologist, 48,* 26–34.

Goodyear, R., Murdock, N., Lichtenberg, J., McPherson, R., Koetting, K., & Petren, S. (2008). Stability and change in counseling psychologists' identities, roles, functions, and career satisfaction across 15 years. *The Counseling Psychologist, 36,* 220–249.

Goodyear, R., & Shaw, M. (Eds.). (1984). Primary prevention on campus and in the community [Special issue]. *Personnel and Guidance Journal, 62*(9), 506–564.

Gordon, R. (1983). An operational classification of disease prevention. *Public Health Reports, 98,* 107–109.

Gullotta, T., & Bloom, M. (Eds.). (2003). *Encyclopedia of primary prevention and health promotion.* New York, NY: Kluwer.

Hage, S., & Romano, J. (2010). History of prevention in groups: Legacy for the 21st century. In R. Conyne & E. Clanton Harpine (Eds.), Prevention groups: Evidence-based approaches to advance the field [Special issue]. *Group Dynamics: Theory, Research, and Practice, 14,* 199–210.

Hage, S., Romano, J., Conyne, R., Kenny, M., Matthews, C., Schwartz, J., & Waldo, M. (2007). Best practice guidelines on prevention practice, research, training, and social advocacy for psychologists. *The Counseling Psychologist, 35,* 493–566.

Health Care and Education Reconciliation Act of 2010, Pub. L. No. 111-152 (March 30, 2010).

Henry, D. B., Farrell, A. D., & the Multisite Violence Prevention Project. (2004). The study designed by a committee: Design of the Multisite Violence Prevention Project. *American Journal of Preventive Medicine, 26*(1), 12–19. doi:10.1016/j.amepre.2003.09.027

Herman, K., Tucker, C., Ferdinand, L., Mirsu-Paun, A., Hansan, N., & Beato, C. (2007). Culturally sensitive health care and counseling psychology: An overview. *The Counseling Psychologist, 35,* 633–649.

Horne, A. M., Bartolomucci, C. L., & Newman-Carlson, D. (2003). *Bully Busters: A teacher's manual for helping bullies, victims, and bystanders (Grades K–5).* Champaign, IL: Research Press.

Horne, A., M., Lind Whitford, J., & Bell, C. J. (2008). *A parent's guide to understanding and responding to bullying: The Bully Busters approach.* Champaign, IL: Research Press.

Ikeda, R., Farrell, A. D., Horne, A. M., Rabiner, D., Tolan P. H., & Reid J. (Eds.). (2004). Prevention of youth violence: The Multisite Violence Prevention Project [Supplement]. *American Journal of Preventive Medicine, 26*(1).

Ingram, R. E. (2005). Clinical training for the next millennium. *Journal of Clinical Psychology, 61,* 1155–1158.

Institute of Medicine. (1994). *Reducing risks for mental disorders: Frontiers for preventive intervention and research.* Washington, DC: National Academy Press.

Kenny, M., Horne, A., Orpinas, P., & Reese (Eds.). (2009). *Realizing social justice: The challenge of preventive interventions.* Washington, DC: American Psychological Association.

Kenny, M., & Romano, J. (2009). Promoting positive development and social justice through prevention: A legacy to the future. In M. Kenny, A. Horne, P. Orpinas, & Reese (Eds.), *Realizing social justice: The challenge of preventive interventions* (pp. 17–36). Washington, DC: American Psychological Association.

Kessler, R. C., Akiskal, H. S., Ames, M., Birnbaum, H., Greenberg, P., Hirschfeld, R. M. A., . . . Wang., P. S. (2006). Prevalence and effects of mood disorders on work performance in a nationally representative sample of U.S. workers. *American Journal of Psychiatry, 163,* 1561–1568.

Kessler, R. C., Berglund, P., Demler, O., Jin, R., Merikangas, K. R., & Walters, E. E. (2005). Lifetime prevalence and age-of-onset distributions of *DSM-IV* disorders in the National Comorbidity Survey replication. *Archives of General Psychiatry, 62,* 593–602.

Kessler, R. C., Chiu, W. T., Demler, O., & Walters, E. E. (2005). Prevalence, severity, and comorbidity of 12-month *DSM-IV* disorders in the National Comorbidity Survey replication. *Archives of General Psychiatry, 62,* 617–627.

Kessler, R. C., Greenberg, P. E., Mickelson, K. D., Meneades, L. M., & Wang, P. S. (2001). The effects of chronic medical conditions on work loss and work cutback. *Journal of Occupational and Environmental Medicine, 43*, 218–225.

Klein, D., & Goldston, S. (Eds.). (1977). *Primary prevention: An idea whose time has come.* Rockville, MD: National Institute of Mental Health.

Lewis, J., & Lewis, M. (1977). *Community counseling: A human services approach* (1st ed.). New York, NY: Wiley.

Lewis, J., & Lewis, M. (1983). *Community counseling: A human services approach* (2nd ed.). New York, NY: Wiley.

Lewis, J., Lewis, M., Daniels, J., & D'Andrea, M. (2003). *Community counseling: Empowerment strategies for a diverse society.* Pacific Grove, CA: Brooks/Cole.

Lopez, S., & Edwards, L. (2008). The interface of counseling psychology and positive psychology: Assessing and promoting strengths. In S. Brown & R. Lent (Eds.), *Handbook of counseling psychology* (pp. 86–102). New York, NY: Wiley.

Lopez, S., Magyar-Moe, J., Petersen, S., Ryder, J., Krieshok, T., O'Byrne, K., . . . Fry, N. (2006). Counseling psychology's focus on positive aspects of human functioning. *The Counseling Psychologist, 34*, 205–227.

Martin, S. (2009). Roadmap for change: An APA task force previews its recommendations for transforming psychology practice to meet the demands of a new world. *Monitor on Psychology, 40*, 66–67.

Matthews, C. (2003, August). Training for prevention competency in counseling Psychology. In M. Kenny (Chair), *Competencies for prevention training incounseling psychology.* Symposium presented at the 111th annual convention of the American Psychological Association, Toronto, Ontario, Canada.

Matthews, C. (2004). *Counseling and prevention: How is the field doing?* Unpublished manuscript.

Matthews, C. R., & Skowron, E. A. (2004). Incorporating prevention into mental health counselor training. *Journal of Mental Health Counseling, 4*, 349–360.

McNeil, B., & Ingram, J. (1983). Prevention and counseling psychology: A survey of training practices. *The Counseling Psychologist, 11*, 95–96.

Meers, B., Werch, C., Hedrick, B., & Lepper, J. (1995). *Prevention training for teachers: A contemporary challenge.* Jacksonville, FL: Center for Alcohol Studies, University of North Florida.

Meyer, A. L., Allison, K. W., Reese, L. E., Gay, F. N., & the Multisite Violence Prevention Project. (2004). Choosing to be violence free in middle school: The student component of the GREAT Schools and Families Universal Program. *American Journal of Preventive Medicine, 26*(1), 20–28. doi:10.1016/j.amepre.2003.09.014

Miller-Johnson, S., Sullivan, T. N., Simon, T. R., & Multisite Violence Prevention Project. (2004). Evaluating the impact of interventions in the Multisite Violence Prevention Study: Samples, procedures, and measures. *American Journal of Preventive Medicine, 26*(1), 48–61. doi:10.1016/j.amepre.2003.09.015

Morrill, W., Oetting, E., & Hurst, J. (1974). Dimensions of counselor functioning. *Personnel and Guidance Journal, 52*, 354–359.

Mrazek, P., & Haggerty, R. (Eds.). (1994). *Reducing risks for mental disorders: Frontiers for preventive intervention.* Washington, DC: National Academy Press.

The Multisite Violence Prevention Project. (2008). The Multisite Violence Prevention Project: Impact of a universal school-based violence prevention program on social-cognitive outcomes. *Preventive Science, 9*, 231–244.

The Multisite Violence Prevention Project. (2009). The ecological effects of universal and selective violence prevention programs for middle school students: A randomized trial. *Journal of Consulting and Clinical Psychology, 77,* 526–542.

Nansel, T. R., Overpeck, M., Pilla, R. S., Ruan, W. J., Simons-Morton, B. G., & Scheidt, P. (2001). Bullying behaviors among US youth: Prevalence and association with psychosocial adjustment. *Journal of the American Medical Association, 285*(16), 2094–2100.

Nash, J. K., & Snyder, S. (2004). Prevention groups. In C. Garvin, L. Gutierrez, & M. Galinky (Eds.), *Handbook of social work with groups* (pp. 176–194). New York, NY: Guilford Press.

Nation, M., Crusto, C., Wandersman, A., Kumpfer, K., Seybolt, Morrissey-Kane, E., & Davino, K. (2003). What works in prevention: Principles of effective prevention programs. *American Psychologist, 58,* 449–456.

National Institute on Drug Abuse. (n.d.). *NIDA InfoFacts: Treatment for drug abusers in the criminal justice system.* Retrieved from http://drugabuse.gov/infofacts/cjtreatment.html

National Prevention Strategy. (2011). Retrieved from www.HealthCare.gov/news/factsheets/prevention06162011a.html, www.HealthCare.gov/center/councils/nphpphc, and http://www.healthcare.gov/prevention/nphpphc/strategy/report.html

Newman, D. A., Horne, A. M., & Bartolomucci, C. L. (2000). *Bully Busters: A teacher's manual for helping bullies, victims, and bystanders (Grades 6-8).* Champaign, IL: Research Press.

O'Byrne, K., Brammer, S., Davidson, M., & Poston, W. (2002). Primary prevention in counseling psychology. *The Counseling Psychologist, 34,* 330–344.

O'Connell, M. E., Boat, T., & Warner, K. E. (Eds.). (2009). *Preventing mental, emotional, and behavioral disorders among young people: Progress and possibilities.* Washington, DC: National Academies Press.

O'Neil, J. M., & Britner, P. A. (2008). Training primary preventionists to make a difference in people's lives. In M. Kenny, A. Horne, P. Orpinas, & L. Reese (Eds.), *Realizing social justice: The challenge of preventive interventions.* Washington, DC: American Psychological Association.

Orpinas, P., & Horne, A. M. (2006). *Bullying prevention: Creating a positive school climate and developing social competence.* Washington, DC: American Psychological Association.

Orpinas, P., Horne, A. M., & the Multisite Violence Prevention Project. (2004). A teacher-focused approach to prevent and reduce students' aggressive behavior: The GREAT Teacher Program. *American Journal of Preventive Medicine, 26*(1), 29–38. doi:10.1016/j.amepre.2003.09.016

Parsons, F. (1909). *Choosing a vocation.* Boston, MA: Houghton Mifflin.

Patient Protection and Affordable Care Act of 2010, Pub. L. No. 111-148 (March 23, 2010).

Phillips, R., Linney, J., & Pack, C. (2008). *Safe School Ambassadors: Harnessing student power to stop bullying and violence.* San Francisco, CA: Jossey-Bass.

Phillips Smith, E., Gorman-Smith, D., Quinn, W. H., Rabiner, D. L., Tolan, P. H., Winn, D.-M., & the Multisite Violence Prevention Project. (2004). Community-based multiple family groups to prevent and reduce violent and aggressive behavior: The GREAT Families Program. *American Journal of Preventive Medicine, 26*(1), 39–47. doi:10.1016/j.amepre.2003.09.018

Prevention. (2011). In *The Oxford English dictionary online version* (3rd ed.). Retrieved from www.oed.com

Price, R. (1983). The education of a preventive psychologist. In R. Felner, L. Jason, J. Moritsugu, & S. Farber (Eds.), *Preventive psychology: Theory, research, and practice* (pp. 290–296). New York, NY: Pergamon.

Price, R., Cowen, E., Lorion, R., & Ramos-McKay, J. (Eds.). (1988). *14 ounces of prevention: A casebook for practitioners.* Washington, DC: American Psychological Association.

Prilleltensky, I. (2012). Wellness as fairness. *American Journal of Community Psychology. 49*, 1-21. doi: 10.1007/s10464-011-9448-8

Prilleltensky, I., & Nelson, G. (1997). Community psychology: Reclaiming social justice. In D. Fox & I. Prillentensky (Eds.), *Critical psychology: An introduction* (pp. 166–184). Thousand Oaks, CA: Sage.

Prochaska, J. O., & Di Clemente, C. C. (1982). Transtheoretical therapy: Toward a more integrative model of change. *Psychotherapy: Theory, Research, and Practice, 19*, 276–288.

Raczynski, K. A., Wetherington, J., Orpinas, P., & Horne, A. M. (2010, August 12–15). *Sixth grade predictors of high school dropout.* Poster Presentation at the 118th annual convention of the American Psychological Association, San Diego, CA.

Rappaport, J. (1977). *Community psychology: Values, research, and action.* New York, NY: Holt, Rinehart, & Winston.

Rappaport, J. (1981). In praise of paradox: A social policy of empowerment over prevention. *American Journal of Community Psychology, 9*, 1–25.

Recommendations of the Task Force for the Use of Groups for Prevention. In R. Conyne (Chair), Division 49. Washington, DC: American Psychological Association.

Reese, L., & Vera, E. (2007). Major contribution: Culturally-relevant prevention: The scientific and practical considerations of community-based programs. *The Counseling Psychologist, 35*, 763–778.

Robers, S., Zhang, J., & Truman, J. (2010). *Indicators of school crime and safety: 2010* (NCES 2011-002/NCJ 230812). Washington, DC: National Center for Education Statistics, U.S. Department of Education, and Bureau of Justice Statistics, Office of Justice Programs, U.S. Department of Justice.

Romano, J., & Hage, S. (2000a). Major contribution: Prevention in counseling psychology. *The Counseling Psychologist, 28*, 733–763.

Romano, J., & Hage, S. (2000b). Prevention: A call to action. *The Counseling Psychologist, 28*, 854–856.

Romano, J., & Hage, S. (2000c). Prevention and counseling psychology: Revitalizing commitments for the 21st century. *The Counseling Psychologist, 28*, 733–763.

Sege, R, & Hoffman, J. (2005). Training health professionals in youth violence prevention. *American Journal of Preventive Medicine (Supplement), 29*, 175–181.

Seligman, M. (2002a). *Authentic happiness: Using the new positive psychology to realize your potential for lasting fulfillment.* New York, NY: Free Press.

Seligman, M. (2002b). Positive psychology, positive prevention, and positive therapy. In C. Snyder & S. Lopez (Eds.), *Handbook of positive psychology* (pp. 3–12). New York, NY: Oxford University Press.

Shaw, M., & Goodyear, R. (Eds.). (1984). Primary prevention in schools [Special issue]. *Personnel and Guidance Journal, 62*(8), 442–495.

Siegel, D. (1999). *The developing mind.* New York, NY: Guilford Press.

Siegel, D. (2010). Reflections on mind, brain, and relationships in group psychotherapy. *International Journal of Group Psychotherapy, 60,* 483–485.

Smith, E. (2006). The strength-based counseling model. *The Counseling Psychologist, 34,* 13–79.

Snyder, C. R., & Elliott, T. R. (2005). Twenty-first century graduate education in clinical psychology: A four level matrix model. *Journal of Clinical Psychology, 61,* 1083–1086.

Snyder, C., & Lopez, S. (Eds.). (2002). *Handbook of positive psychology.* New York, NY: Oxford University Press.

Snyder, C., & Lopez, S. (Eds.). (2007). *Positive psychology: The scientific and practical explorations of human strengths.* Thousand Oaks, CA: Sage.

Spreight, S., & Vera, E. (2008). Social justice and counseling psychology: A challenge to the profession. In S. Brown & R. Lent (Eds.), *Handbook of counseling psychology* (pp. 54–67). New York, NY: Wiley.

A thin line. (n.d.). Retrieved from http://www.athinline.org

Tober, N. (1993). Updated meta analysis of adolescent drug prevention programs. In C. Montoya, C. Ringwalt, B. Ryan, & R. Zimmerman (Eds.), *Evaluating school-lined prevention strategies: Alcohol, tobacco, and other drugs* (pp. 71–86). San Diego, CA: UCSD Extension, University of California.

Tobler, N., & Stratton, H. (1997). Effectiveness of school based drug prevention programs: A meta-analysis of the research. *Journal of Primary Prevention, 18,* 71–128.

Toporek, R., Gerstein, L., Fouad, N., Roysircar, G., & Israel, T. (Eds.). (2006). *Handbook for social justice in counseling psychology: Leadership, vision, and action.* Thousand Oaks, CA: Sage.

U.S. Surgeon General. (1979). *Healthy People: The Surgeon General's Report on Health Promotion and Disease Prevention.* Washington, DC: Office of Disease Prevention and Health Promotion, Department of Health and Humans Services.

U.S. Surgeon General. (1990). *Healthy People: The Surgeon General's Report on Health Promotion and Disease Prevention.* Washington, DC: Office of Disease Prevention and Health Promotion, Department of Health and Humans Services.

U.S. Surgeon General. (2000). *Healthy People: The Surgeon General's Report on Health Promotion and Disease Prevention.* Washington, DC: Office of Disease Prevention and Health Promotion, Department of Health and Humans Services.

U.S. Surgeon General. (2010). *Healthy People: The Surgeon General's Report on Health Promotion and Disease Prevention.* Washington, DC: Office of Disease Prevention and Health Promotion, Department of Health and Humans Services.

Vera, E. (2000). A recommitment to prevention work in counseling psychology. *The Counseling Psychologist, 28,* 829–837.

Vera, E. (Ed.). (2012). *Oxford handbook of prevention.* New York, NY: Oxford University Press.

Vera, E., Buhim, L., & Isacco, A. (2009). The role of prevention in psychology's social justice agenda. In M. Kenny, A. Horne, P. Orpinas, & L. Reese (Eds.), *Realizing social justice: The challenge of preventive intervention* (pp. 79–96). Washington, DC: American Psychological Association.

Vera, E., & Spreight, S. (2003). Multicultural competence, social justice, and counseling psychology: Expanding our roles. *The Counseling Psychologist, 31,* 253–272.

Versel, N. (2010, June 6). *Smartphone apps serve as "electronic therapist" for mental health patients*. Retrieved from www.fiercemobilehealthcare.com/

Waldo, M., Schwartz, J., Horne, A., & Cote, L. (2011). Prevention groups. In R. Conyne (Ed.), *Oxford handbook of group counseling* (pp. 452–468). New York, NY: Oxford University Press.

Wang, P. H., Lane, M., Olfson, M., Pincus, H. A., Wells, K. B., & Kessler, R. C. (2005). Twelve-month use of mental health services in the United States: Results from the National Comorbidity Survey replication. *Archives of General Psychiatry, 62,* 629–640.

Watkins, C., Lopez, F., Campbell, V., & Himmel, C. (1986). Contemporary counseling psychology: Results of a national survey. *Journal of Counseling Psychology, 33,* 301–309.

Western Interstate Commission for Higher Education. (1972). *The ecosystem model: Designing campus environments*. Boulder, CO: Author.

Wetherington, J., Raczynski, K. A., Orpinas, P., & Horne, A. M. (2010, August 12–15). *Latent profile analysis based on teacher ratings of sixth graders*. Poster presentation at the 118th annual convention of the American Psychological Association, San Diego, CA.

Whiteley, J. (Ed.). (1980). *The history of counseling psychology*. Monterey, CA: Brooks/Cole.

WHO World Mental Health Survey Consortium. (2004). Prevalence, severity, and unmet need for treatment of mental disorders in the World Health Organization World Mental Health surveys. *Journal of American Medical Association, 291,* 2581–2590.

Zolik, E. (1983). Training for preventive psychology in community and academic settings. In R. Felner, L. Jason, J. Moritsugu, & S. Farber (Eds.), *Preventive psychology: Theory, research, and practice* (pp. 273–289). New York, NY: Pergamon.

Index _____

About the Authors _____

Robert K. Conyne, PhD, Professor Emeritus from the University of Cincinnati, is a Licensed Psychologist, Clinical Counselor, and Fellow of the Association for Specialists in Group Work (ASGW) and the American Psychological Association (APA). He has 36 years of professional experience as a University Professor and Department Head, counselor, administrator, consultant, and trainer. Dr. Conyne has received many awards, including Eminent Career Award from the ASGW; Lifetime Achievement Award in Prevention, Society of Counseling Psychology of the APA; Distinguished Alumni Award of Distinction from Purdue University; and has served as a Soros International Scholar. He was President of the APA's Division of Group Psychology and Group Psychotherapy and also of the American Counseling Association's ASGW. With more than 200 scholarly publications and presentations including 12 books in his areas of expertise (group work, prevention, and ecological counseling), along with broad international consultation in these areas—most recently with U.S. military personnel—Dr. Conyne is recognized as an expert in working with people and systems. With colleague (and wife), Lynn S. Rapin, PhD, he also helps people plan and prepare psychologically for their upcoming retirement, using the holistic approach they developed, "Charting Your Personal Future." The edited *Oxford Handbook of Group Counseling* (2011) is his most recent offering, preceded by *Prevention Program Development and Evaluation* (Sage), and 10 other books. When not working, he and Lynn—as often as possible with their children Suzanne (married to Pete) and Zack—can be found traveling or enjoying life at their Northern Ontario cottage with their dog, Lucy.

Arthur M. Horne, PhD, Dean of Education and Distinguished Research Professor Emeritus at the University of Georgia, is a Licensed Psychologist and is a Fellow of the Association for Specialists in Group Work (ASGW) and the American Psychological Association (APA), as well as several divisions of APA. He has more than 40 years of professional experience as a university professor, department head, program coordinator for counseling psychology and for marriage and family therapy programs, and as a consultant and trainer. Dr. Horne has received recognition for his work, including

APA's Society of Counseling Psychology Awards for Social Justice, Psychology Faces of Counseling Psychology, and the Lifetime Achievement Award in Prevention. He has received the Extended Research Award from the American Counseling Association (ACA), the Eminent Career Award from the ASGW, Distinguished Alumni Award from Southern Illinois University, and has served as a Soros Open Society International Scholar. He was President of the APA's Division of Group Psychology and Group Psychotherapy and also of the American Counseling Association's ASGW. He is president-elect of the APA Division 17, Society of Counseling Psychology. He has more than 200 scholarly publications and presentations, including 9 coauthored and 5 coedited books in his areas of expertise (group work, prevention, bullying and violence reduction, and marriage and family counseling), along with broad international consultation in these areas. He and his wife take pleasure in travels and particularly spending time on the Oregon coast to enjoy the ocean, mountains, rivers, and abundance of nature.

Katherine Raczynski, PhD, is a graduate of the the Department of Educational Psychology and Instructional Technology in the College of Education at the University of Georgia where she earned a PhD in educational psychology. She has worked in the field of adolescent violence prevention as part of the Healthy Teens and the Multisite Violence Prevention Projects, a 7-year series of studies investigating students' social development as they transition from middle school to high school. She has also worked with students, teachers, and parents to reduce bullying and aggression in schools as part of the Bully Busters program, and is coauthor of three forthcoming books in the Bully Busters publication series. She is the recipient of the 2009 APA Society of Counseling Psychology Prevention Section Graduate Student Prevention Research Award and Research Proposal Award, the 2010 APA Division 16 School Psychology Award for Outstanding Student Scholarship, and she was named a 2011 David Watts Scholar by the Southeast Regional Association of Teacher Educators. In her free time, she enjoys cooking, traveling, reading, and spending time with family.

§SAGE research**methods**

The essential online tool for researchers from the world's leading methods publisher

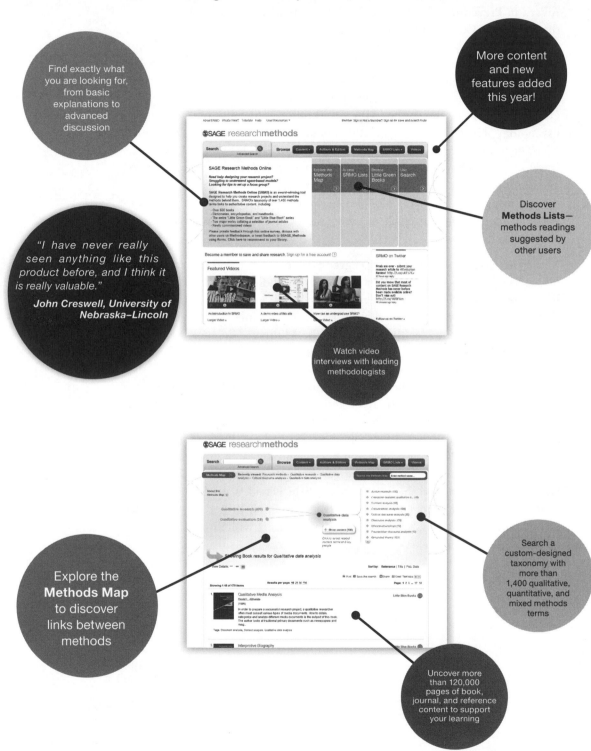

Find exactly what you are looking for, from basic explanations to advanced discussion

More content and new features added this year!

"I have never really seen anything like this product before, and I think it is really valuable."

John Creswell, University of Nebraska–Lincoln

Discover **Methods Lists**— methods readings suggested by other users

Watch video interviews with leading methodologists

Explore the **Methods Map** to discover links between methods

Search a custom-designed taxonomy with more than 1,400 qualitative, quantitative, and mixed methods terms

Uncover more than 120,000 pages of book, journal, and reference content to support your learning

Find out more at
www.sageresearchmethods.com